AF290360

PhD Confessions

From Democracy Scholars, Students, and Supporters

edited by Lea Heyne & Christian Ewert

DemocracyNet

Bibliografische Information der Deutschen Nationalbibliothek
Die Deutsche Nationalbibliothek verzeichnet diese Publikation
in der Deutschen Nationalbibliografie; detaillierte bibliografische
Daten sind im Internet über http://dnb.d-nb.de abrufbar

DemocracyNet is a non-profit organization located in Switzerland
https://democracynet.eu
info@democracynet.eu

Layout: Christian Ewert

Printed by BoD – Books on Demand, Norderstedt

ISBN: 978-3-75624-112-5

Content

Part C
Accompanying a PhD

Introduction

Christian Ewert

ewert.ch@gmail.com

I remember well the day I met Lea. We both had just started our PhD in democracy studies as part of the third (and final) phase of the NCCR Democracy, which was a high profile research collaboration of several scholars and universities in Switzerland funded by the Swiss National Science Foundation.

Once a year in winter, NCCR Democracy's members met in the beautiful city of Thun in the Bernese Highlands to discuss and exchange their findings and thoughts. You must imagine the atmosphere at these meetings. In Thun, just below its castle and between its medieval buildings, the river Aare leaves a crystal clear lake. There are hills and forests, and many cozy bars and pubs and restaurants. In the distance, you can see the mighty mountains of the Swiss alps. And on the inside, in the conference room, we saw the men and women who constitute the community of Swiss democracy scholars. A fitting scene on so many levels, perhaps.

If memory serves well, Lea was sitting to my left on the day we met, right next to the window that reached from floor to ceiling. We chatted a bit, got to know each other somewhat, but mostly listened to the presentations and discussions. In the evening, we went with the others to have beer and wine and cocktails. It was fun.

That day was nine years ago. In the meantime, Lea successfully defended her PhD and I mine. We both did some teaching, some research, some publications. She's still working as an academic scholar today, while I focus mostly on teaching and coaching. She traveled the world and I was adopted by cats. In short, we both went on with our respective life journeys inside and outside of academia. But regardless of our own individual life paths, we never lost contact. Sure, there were times when we didn't talk for a year or so. But we are members of the same academic NGO[1] and met at workshops or other events. And in a way, there was always something to talk about.

Of course, during our time as PhD researchers and thereafter, we had some good and some not so good experiences. We made some friends. We did some things right and (maybe too many) others wrong. And for many reasons, this time had and still has a tremendous impact on our lives, on the way we think and engage, on how we and others see us.

On the one hand, Lea and I have to be honest and say that we were very privileged during our PhD studies. We were located in Switzerland, a very rich, safe and welcoming country, had supportive peers and friends, received (in comparison) generous salaries and project funding, and were part of a helpful and comprehensive doctoral program.

On the other hand, we can also honestly say that we did struggle. And that we had to face both internal challenges – such as anxieties and doubts – as well as external ones – some of which related to our scientific work, others to our social and institutional environment.

And over the most recent years, we found that sharing our experiences in an open, respectful and authentic

1 That is DemocracyNet, which also serves as the publisher of this book.

way is so helpful on many levels.[2] Sharing with a person
you trust will remove that weight from your shoulders
and can rekindle that inner flame of yours. And listening
to others will help you relate your own experiences
with those of another person. Indeed, sharing personal
stories, our narratives, is such a powerful endeavor
that it has become central to many approaches in
therapy[3] and personal growth and development[4].

And in a nutshell, this is what this book is all about:
people sharing their stories. People who are currently
working at university to obtain a PhD and those who
already got one. People who struggled quite a bit with
their PhD, and those who enjoyed their time. People
who still work in academia and others who left. So all
kinds of people, and all kinds of stories, really.

It is important to say here that we didn't want to publish
an academic book. You will find no hypotheses in
here, no methods section, and the included stories
are anecdotal but certainly not representative
of the larger universe of PhD experiences.

Instead, we wanted to give space to people to share in an
authentic, personal, and maybe even intimate voice. This
is why we asked for *confessions* and chose the book's title
accordingly. The word confessions should not imply that our
authors did something wrong, or have sinned in any way.
There is nothing that they need to be ashamed of, nothing for

---

2 Brown, Brené (2012). *Daring Greatly*. London: Penguin Books.

3 White, Cheryl & Denborough, David (1998). *Introducing Narrative Therapy*. Adelaide:
Dulwich Centre Publications.

4 Stelter, Reinhard (2012). *A Guide to Third Generation Coaching*. Dordrecht: Springer.

them to come clean about. But we wanted to encourage them to write honestly, to acknowledge the right and the wrong, the pleasure and the pain, and maybe even say things that have been left unspoken so far. And Lea and I are so grateful to the authors, and deeply moved and inspired by their stories.

The book has three parts. In the first one, people tell stories about what studying democracy means to them. Since they are dedicating their career to this topic, we asked them to write about *how* and *why* they decided democracy to be worth studying. What is it that makes democracy interesting? How has the dedication to study it professionally affected their lives?

For the book's second part, we asked people to share about their experiences as PhD researchers. And it was our goal to include diverse experiences. Sure, to some degree doing a PhD is a similar process for everybody – you have to spend several years of your life working on one topic, writing about it, and then defending your thesis. However, since we are all individuals with our very own strengths and weaknesses, needs, and hopes, and since we are subject to often diverging external conditions, this process affects all of us differently.

The third and final part of the book includes stories from people who support others in doing a PhD. These people are supervisors, coaches, language trainers and editors, among others. And they offer their own unique perspectives on the PhD process, which are informed by working with many PhD researchers over many years.

Before we will finally start with the stories, from the very first time we talked about this book, Lea and I agreed that it should be about sharing. And while we and the authors share our stories with you in this book, we want to encourage you to share your stories with us as well. So please, get in touch with us as well as the authors if you feel that a story resonates with you, or you have specific questions or remarks for someone. You will find email addresses throughout this book, and all of us would be delighted to hear from you and listen to your story.

Part A

*

Studying Democracy

In this section we want to present accessible first-hand impressions of what it means to do research on democracy. Of course, there are many great books out there on what democracy means and how we can study it, and we don't want to (and really can't) compete with those. Instead, we wanted more personal stories on how researchers think about democracy, and why they decided to dedicate their work to this topic. So, we asked colleagues who work on different aspects of democracy, with different methods and different backgrounds, to tell us their stories. We asked philosophers as well as empiricists. Scholars who work on Europe, on Africa, on China. Scholars who always wanted to work on democracy, and those who never planned to. How did they come to study democracy? What does democracy mean to them? Which aspects of democracy do they find most important, or most interesting? What are the challenges that arise when studying democracy? Which literature would they recommend to young PhD students? And what would they have liked to know when they started working on democracy?

(1) Out of the Nether and Into Ruin: Existentialism, Democratic Theory and "Singing" Possibilities into Creation

Jean-Paul Gagnon
jean-paul.gagnon@canberra.edu.au

1. A glacier shifts and its voice, a chthonic base, bellows down the valley. I feel it boom through my lungs. – A sense of permeability with *Aoraki*

2. The red desert – chilling under HD stars, devastatingly hot under a HiFi sun – leaves its fine dust on my boots. I never wipe it off and hope it stays forever. – Wishes with *Uluru*

3. What powerful wind! "Hail the Southern Sea!" I yell from the depth of my ass. Columns of black basalt look like wrecked spaceships in the wild blue, immense crashing waves, and swirling whites of an ocean connecting me with Antarctica. – Relationality in *Wirangu Country*

4. They're called the "Remarkable Rocks". What a colonial insult to the petrified remains of a creator, a god, who died here to make the milky way. Here, in the men's place, sloping out to sea … here is the first time I am not bothered by the thought of joining him. This place is pure liminality. – Translucence(?) in *Karta Pintingga*

5. "We exit into life and enter into death" wrote Lao Tze in *The Book of Virtues*. Somewhere in this space interpolated by two moments that we did/did not, and will/will not, control

is perhaps the greatest puzzle: why are we here? – "Stuck in the middle with you" in *T'koronto, now with concrete!*

*

Out of the nether and into ruin
I did not train in any of the hallmark institutions of our calling. A call to understand, a call to make it better, a call to question, a call to fight. What I know now, what I have been through in the pursuit of trying to understand democracy as a scholar initially on the outside, busy in the peripheries, has rendered me unsuitable for anything else. Unable to take orders (Pausch, 2019) and drawn to "compounding complexity" (Barnett, 2000), I am ruin to the managerial-authoritarian, to the consumer-capitalist, to the male-traditionalist, to the hyperproductive-egoist, to the imperialist-ivyleaguer. So, I suppose as countless poker players have said: "I'm all in." The only difference between I and those considering their cards is choice – it doesn't feel to me as if I ever "chose" to study democracy, to push my chips at democratic theory, or to fold my hand in the face of bad odds – I unwittingly played it every time. A career in democracy studies just happened through luck and guile. Or maybe instinct and perseverance. Or just through old-fashioned fate – in this universe, timeline and life at least. As Walter Scott, one of my favourite writers (because of *Ivanhoe*, always Ivanhoe!), wrote: "We shall never learn to feel and respect our real calling and destiny, unless we have taught ourselves to consider every thing as moonshine, compared with the education of the heart".

My parents could have passed for professors (I am a "first gen" academic). They were instructive in their own, quite different, ways. My mother, Celina, and her three older sisters Stasia, Dominika and Marina, were for example taught to smuggle goods (textiles, fruit, clothing, even wallpaper) across the Soviet Blocs by my grandmother, Monika. Only through this blackmarket trade could enough money be made for a few of them to pay their way out of communism and land in the social-capitalistic architecture of West Germany. Once, now back in time and back in the Bloc, on a train heading from Budapest to Bucharest (suitcase full of harmless contraband), my mother, exhausted, fell into a catatonic sleep. She awoke finding that her legs were propped on a dapper young man's arms (he was seated opposite) who, so astounded for being used as a post by a young lady, didn't dare budge for some hours for fear of waking her. My mother recently told the story and remarked: "thank god I was wearing pants!" Once, on a train platform at night, a rough drunk man grabbed my mother, threw her over his shoulder, and started taking her away. She couldn't struggle free. He was brought down by a high heel to the head. Stasia had clobbered him in the fierce rescue of her younger sister. The dangerous adventures these young women undertook brings Ginger Rogers to mind: "she did everything he [Fred Astaire] could do [but] backwards! And in high heels!"[1]

Like so many other Polish people, my family (mother's side) had somehow endured their country being partitioned four times in the last two centuries – the most recent having been done by Hitler and Stalin, or the Black and the Red Deaths.[2] There are stories of my grandparents hiding basic

____

1 A quote from the American cartoonist Bob Thames.

2 A line borrowed from Andrew Tarnowski in his 2007 book The Last Mazurka. NYC: St Martin's Press.

materials (wood, paint) from the military requisitions of invasive armies. I wear my great-grandfather's ring – he was a major in the Polish cavalry. He survived the Great War but was captured and shot somewhere, it is rumoured, near Berlin mere days after the armistice. So, an intimate knowledge of dispossession of private property, oppression by the state and by men, occupation and mockery, being murdered in fending off occupying forces, the experience of puppet states, and the discomforts of poverty whose escape was only to be won through terrible risk taking, would come to suffuse my means for perception. Everywhere is the question of power. Everywhere is the question of choice. Are we top, or bottom, or irrelevant? Are we going to struggle for "democracy" (of some type or another even under an altogether different sign like "manapori") or are we going to take the easy route and be the authority or be subsumed by it?

Prior to entering university, I wanted to know why the world (my understanding of reality) hurt and what we could do about it. Of course, I didn't articulate it in that way at the time and only understand what I was doing now – with decades-worth of vantage points to look upon my past. And then there was the fascination with lizards – I would bring them to the table in my shirt pocket as guests for dinner – which no one could explain. I guess all that remains true to this day as I am presently drawn to both linguistic (human) and nonhuman sources of democracy.

Undergrad unusual, and then Korea
My undergraduate, major in global history and a smattering of concentrations in political science/languages/environmental science, happened across three universities in Ontario: Carlton (first year), Toronto (second year) and Trent (third

year) where I finished. Uncertain as to where I would go
from there, I happened on an offer to join a group of fresh
graduates who would come to teach English in South Korea
as part of a public-private-partnership between the South
Korean government and the LG corporation. Theirs would
be among the first subsidized schools in the country for the
provision of afterschool English lessons to children from
poorer families. We were to live in a specially built dormitory
for teachers located behind the school. It backed onto a long,
sylvan, range of wooded hills. It turned out the dormitory
wasn't finished its construction when we were due to start
our lessons and the school's budget was tight. So, unable to
afford "proper accommodation", we were housed in a brothel
for a month. I was on the "neon green floor", would buy a
refreshing small cola from a vending machine that touted
other amusements, awoke each morning to many lewd (few
tasteful) calling cards from sex workers which were, without
fail, pushed under the door each night as I slept. It was then, in
this environment (resonating with Howard Becker here), that
I composed a PhD proposal which I sent for consideration to
Australia. I remember ticking a small box in the application
that would have me be considered for a "commonwealth
scholars program", or some phrasing like that, and then
promptly forgot about the application altogether. I instructed
English from the music room (having played the piano
with two hands and a foot, I was photographed for the local
papers) and the "game show" room, much in the feels at the
time with Alex Trebek of *Jeopardy!* I would hike afterwards,
or before breakfast, in the wooded hills alongside elderly
residents and soldiers undertaking their training.

***Postgrad* "on the road"**

I found out, on holiday from teaching in the Borneo jungle
(Sarawak, through satellite connection), that I would be
accepted with a full scholarship into the doctoral program
at the Queensland University of Technology (QUT). They
had sent, they explained, my acceptance letter for the
application I had forgotten about to the wrong person and,
instead of giving me the same amount of time to organise
myself, required a move (which turned out to be via Malaysia,
South Korea, Canada, the USA, Fiji and finally Australia)
within mere weeks. It also turned out I did not qualify for the
doctoral entry at QUT and had to begin as a Master's student
instead. I could then, after a year of study and research,
present a proposal to transform the Master's pathway into a
PhD programme. They call this an "articulation". So, I have
been awarded a BA and a PhD with no Honour's or Master's
in between. It was around this time that the University
announced it would close the School of Humanities and
Social Sciences, where I was based, and the Faculty began
to leave. Whilst both of my supervisors were spared the
chop, the culture was gone, and I began to wander in
search of other universities, other people, to learn with.

This itineracy, working between an assortment of
universities and institutions of governance (like the
International Labour Organization where I interned
in my second year of candidacy), would turn out to be
the defining characteristic of my PhD period but also
for some years thereafter until receiving an invitation
to accept a five-year postdoctoral fellowship in
Melbourne with the Australian Catholic University.

When it came time to submit the thesis, the examination
took six months. The first examiner recommended minor
changes. This was Ian Cook (Murdoch University), who
passed away recently, too young. He shared his role as
examiner with me as we were taking the lift to a seminar
room during an Australian political science conference. The
other examiner, David Lovell (UNSW ADFA), recommended
outright rejection of the thesis and resubmission at the
master's level. It's still not clear to me why my work was sent
to him for review, nor why he accepted this undertaking, as
I've since not come across an overlap between his work and
my own. A third examiner was sought and came back with
minor changes. I would come to find out, many years later,
that this third examiner was Mary Walsh, my colleague whose
office is next door to mine at the University of Canberra.

What caught me further by surprise is that my student visa for
Australia expired the day I submitted for examination and I
was forced to move onto a tourist visa with only a small cash
reserve as my scholarship was meagre, just under 20,000.00
AUD a year (below the poverty line). The only way to keep
myself whilst the examination took place was to work on
the black, in a friend's fish and chips shop, where I was paid
in cash after each day's labour. This was not the start I had
envisioned – primed, as I was, by senior colleagues with the
understanding that academic jobs would *come to me*. And
so began the anticlimactic experience of receiving a PhD,
obtaining the title of Dr, and then reliance on the goodwill of
others (mainly my family) to keep me housed, fed, and able
to apply for more than a hundred jobs around the globe. None
of which eventuated. The PhD consequently felt worthless to
me. Once I was proud of what I was doing with it and at once
I was happy to leave it behind, to write my first book instead,

typed at my childhood's dining table and grandmother's desk
in my parent's home. I never did publish out of the thesis,
mere "driver's licence" as it came to be for me. I still don't
open it and keep it buried behind other people's books.

The pandemic years

Let's leapfrog the many years from then until corona-now.
Some of what has transpired includes numerous, always
rewarding, collaborations[3] and a polite hand-signed letter
of refusal from Habermas (I had invited him to an interview
for my second book). There was a postdoc and it did "come
to me" as my supervisors had assured – so they were right.
This was followed by securing a permanent "core" faculty
position at a young ambitious university (Canberra),
months in hospital as a caretaker, a divorce, thousands of
students taught across nearly a dozen subjects given at all
levels, too much travel (sorry, environment, like almost
every other prof I hurt you in pursuit of my career), weird
and confusing spats with management (where absurdity
does indeed intersect with fascism), ambrosian new love,
getting to know my ageing parents, now I'm an uncle,
and bearing witness to the exit from academia of far too
many colleagues by their choice (Boredom? Done with
the pretence of publishing and over-inflated promises of
readership?), or by the over-institutionalised hand of "HR"
(human rancidness?), or by simple and honest exhaustion.

Through this slipslide between highs and lows and bearing
the overlap of goods and bads has come many lessons for
the study of democracy (we will come to these next). There

---

3 With Noam Chomsky, David Held (twice, vale), Robin Eckersley, Francis
Fukuyama, Ulrich Beck (vale), John Dryzek, John Keane, John Dunn, Albert Weale,
Wolfgang Merkel, Thomas Seeley, Ramin Jahanbegloo, Simon Tormey,
Sue Donaldson, Janneke Vink, Frederic Schaffer, Samuel Moyn, and Wade Davis,
among others.

is also a crackshot of rippling sound that, like lightning, or, sometimes much slower, like a muezzin calling to prayer or a long dull foghorn, comes alive inside the nurtured parliament, the cranial counsel, the socialized schizophrenia (an inner democracy in training) of my mental experience. The sound I would like to share with you comes from the anthropologist and ethnobotanist Wade Davis. He told me, in a collaboration that spanned the first few variants of the virus, how different indigenous persons tell stories, sing songs, and dance to quite literally do their part to bring the world into creation. Their stories are world-makers, their dances show routes into the future, their songs keep history living as an is and not necessarily a desiccated was.

What this revealed to me is the power of story-telling, fiction, ritual, narration, constantly struggling for the right ethics in action, communication, and community, but ultimately a sensitive attention to where you are. Our time between exit into life and entry into death can be given to being kind and doing all that we can to offer alternative (better) worlds for habitation, different possibilities for the human spirit to explore, and hopefully shifts of culture into directions that reduce unnecessary suffering and that make the unavoidable suffering of life that much easier to bear in the gracious company of loving others. This cannot be done in the abstract: it is a lived practise and requires an attentiveness to how you (mind, body, soul, gut, instinct, whatever) perceive reality and how we can, and are, to do so together. *Perceive* first, sense your reality, do not mistake your perception as universal (it only applies to you), and let this embodied, material, experience fill you up with lessons, inspirations, ideas and routes for action.

Counsel for friends and strangers alike

So what is democracy, then, and why should one bother studying it? Democracy is a choice: whoever you are, wherever you are, even if completely alone, you will always have the choice to do something with a gentle sensitivity to the needs of others (such as those others that inhabit your mind), without harassing them or being unkind to them, involving everyone who wants to be involved, without silencing anyone, with toleration, without applying force upon them, taking the time to figure things out in a way that reduces harm (especially those unintended harms that may cascade into the future). This looks simple in proposition but it is astoundingly difficult to achieve. For millennia humans have been working out how to avoid the simplicity, the convenience, of authoritarianism, of a life where there are a few people who have the power and who order everyone else about with only limited mechanisms of control for "the masses" to have some say, or some placatory semblance of it, over their collective destiny.

I am, for example, presently working on a book called "democracy therapy" which proposes the democratisation (through one or more forms of democracy as may be applicable or preferable to persons in their respective situations) of our social lives. Think of families, schools, workplaces, civic associations like hospitals, retirement homes, prisons, the military, and even our relationships with ourselves: everywhere you look, even in the world's most celebrated "progressive" countries, there is predominantly authoritarianism. I am the parent or guardian, I am the teacher, I am the boss, I am the doctor or manager or warden or commander, I am singular, decisive, and rule my inner-kingdom with an iron will (lest I be caught talking to myself). Theoretically, this book has been unproblematic to write:

the literature and my own personal life experiences are full
of good arguments and qualitative evidence (quantitative
statistics are underdeveloped) about how democratic families,
schools, workplaces, hospitals (etc.), and selves are better than
their authoritarian (status quo) renditions. But the practice,
and I am practising Hubert Hermans' "inner democracy" for
it is only here that I have the power to do so (how ironic for
a prof of democracy), is jarring in its difficulty. Everywhere
I turn in my discussions and propositions with people from
various walks of life, even from a pro-democracy activist,
there is *hesitancy* and outright *refusal*. To the activist, who I
met at an online Arab-Russo democracy summit, I proposed
some practices of family democracy such as putting the UN
charter of the rights of the child on her children's bedroom
wall and explaining their rights to them. Her response: "no
way". My sense is that she feared her family would disintegrate
without her boss-strength at the helm. Perhaps it is the
same feeling for elites ruling their respective societies.

I will end, then, by saying that democracy has to be studied
because we are not democratic. We do not actually live in
democracies. We reside in its name only. To be told that you
live in a "full democracy" is a sham as most of us, from the
time of our birth, will be conditioned into systems of non-
democracy: of conformity, obeyance, and deference. Our
unique spirits, that which makes us all of equal worth and
of equal awe (alongside all other nonhuman entities with
spirits of their own), are subsumed into something else:
into the manufactured "normal" of the bosses who cannot
tolerate your rebellion and so you are punished, who do not
permit your individuality and so you are banished, who deny
you your becoming, who mistreat you and yet you must stay,

who insult you but you have to ask for more – because where else can we go in a capitalistic world of financial scarcity?

We, in the study of democracy, are like monks and must proselytize (see, for example, Dean, Gagnon and Asenbaum 2019). We are like pastors and must lead by example (Fleuss, 2021). Ours is not a profession although we are professionals. To study democracy is to sense your reality. You must have the capacity to see through constructs, to soften your hands, to open your mind to the chorus of possibilities, and to ask: Where does it hurt? What can we do (Warren, 2017), what can we design (Saward, 2021), to make it better? Everywhere there will be work for you to do. Just look around: democracy is a whisper, a possibility, a shadow, a hint, a horizon, and maybe even the greatest lie the 20th century ever told. Democracy is more than elections (although that form from its many forms is important too) and so much more than the sobriquet handed out to countries by institutions of measurement.

Find me a society where the democratic family (Tamura 2020), school (Giroux 2014, Mitropolski 2014), workplace (Frega 2020), civic institutions (e.g. retirement homes, prisons, hospitals, see: Ercan and Dzur 2016), and selves (Hermans 2020) are in the majority. Or, more realistically, let's keep trying to create that society wherever it is that we happen to find ourselves or in those places that we call our own. You don't need to be a professor to do this, but you probably do need to be ruined like me.

Recommended reading
- Jane Bennett. 2004. "The Force of Things: Steps Toward an Ecology of Matter". *Political Theory*, 32 (3): 347-372.

- John Keane. 2022. *The Shortest History of Democracy.* Melbourne: Black Inc Books.
- Thomas Seeley. 2010. *Honeybee Democracy.* Princeton: Princeton University Press.
- Ongoing ECPR short essay series on the "science of democracy": https://theloop.ecpr.eu/page/1/?s=

References

Barnett, Ronald. 2000. "University Knowledge in an Age of Supercomplexity". *Higher Education,* 40: 409-422.

Dean, Rikki, Jean-Paul Gagnon, and Hans Asenbaum. 2019. "What Is Democratic Theory?" *Democratic Theory,* 6(2): 5-20.

Ercan, Selen and Albert Dzur. 2016. "Participatory in Unlikely Places: What Democratic Theorists Can Learn From Democratic Professionals". *Democratic Theory,* 3(2): 94-113.

Fleuss, Dannica. 2021. *Radical Proceduralism: Democracy from Philosophical Principles to Political Institutions.* Bingley: Emerald Group.

Frega, Roberto. 2020. "Against Analogy: Why Analogical Arguments in Support of Workplace Democracy Must Necessarily Fail". *Democratic Theory,* 7(1): 1-26.

Giroux, Henry A. 2014. "The Swindle of Democracy in the Neoliberal University and the Responsibility of Intellectuals". *Democratic Theory,* 1(1): 9-37.

Hermans, Hubert. 2020. *Inner Democracy: Empowering the Mind Against a Polarizing Society.* Oxford: Oxford University Press.

Mitropolitski, Simeon. 2014. "The Role of Schools in the Rise of Egalitarian Political Culture". *Democratic Theory*, 1(1): 38-57.

Pausch, Markus. 2019. "Democracy Needs Rebellion: A Democratic Theory Inspired by Camus". *Theoria: A Journal of Social and Political Theory*, 66(161), pp. 91-107.

Saward, Michael. 2021. *Democratic Design*. Oxford: Oxford University Press.

Tamura, Tetsuki. 2020. "Another Way for Deepening Democracy Without Shortcuts". *Journal of Deliberative Democracy*, 16(2): 89-95.

Warren, Mark E. 2017. "A Problem-based Approach to Democratic Theory". *American Political Science Review*, 111(1): 39-53.

(2) Why Study African Democracy?

Edalina Rodrigues Sanches
ersanches@@ics.ulisboa.pt

Kantádu ma dimokrasiâ
Ma stába sukundidu
Ma tudu dja sai na kláru
I nós tudu dja bira sabidu

Dimokránsa, Song by Mayra Andrade (Cabo Verdean Singer)[1]

*

My interest in democracy, as a research topic, started while I was a BA student in Sociology at the Faculty of Social and Human Sciences, New University of Lisbon, in the early 2000s. Navigating through the works of Pierre Bourdieu, Norbert Elias and many others, I was captivated by rather existential questions such as: how did we get here? Can we build different (political) societies? Is there room for change and invention? These were some of the questions that puzzled me back then – and somehow they still do – and they are not unrelated with who I am as researcher, teacher, and supervisor.

Circling back to how it all started, I must say that it was only after I attended the discipline Political Sociology that I

---

1 English Translation: It was said that democracy / Was like a hidden treasure / But now that it has been found / We have all opened our eyes. Democracy, Song by Mayra Andrade (Full lyrics and translation available here: https://lyricstranslate.com/en/dimokr%C3%A1nsa-lopsided-democracy.html, 16-06-2022)

decided to focus on politics, and more specifically democratic transitions, as the research topic for my BA dissertation. The country case study was not immediately evident, but I eventually decided to focus on Cabo Verde, my parents' home country. My supervisor at the time argued that there was a gap of studies on African countries, and more specifically, former Portuguese colonies. To be honest I was not fully convinced with studying democratisation. To start, as a Sociology student I was not comfortable with the literature on political transitions and democratisation. Additionally, as a daughter of immigrants, who hardly discussed or engaged in politics, and who did not enjoy full political rights, I was rather disenchanted with democracy. Therefore, doing the BA dissertation on Cabo Verde's democratic transition helped me to understand democracy better.

Since then I have been working on democratisation in Africa focusing on parties, party systems, elections, popular protest and representation. During the Masters in Comparative Politics at the Institute of Social Sciences, University of Lisbon I have researched party system institutionalisation in Cabo Verde, and how this was an important element for democratisation. Arguably, the two processes may not necessarily move along together, but the interesting thing about Cabo Verde is that it revealed that, sometimes, stable party systems could be paired with strong democratic institutions, pro-democratic elites and relatively high levels of citizens' participation in politics.

Subsequently, when I started my PhD in Political Science in 2009 at the University of Lisbon, I continued to focus on party system institutionalisation[2]. I first collected data on hundreds of elections across 19 democratic and hybrid regimes in Africa to chart and explain electoral trends and party system characteristics since the start of democratic experiments in Africa up until 2011. I then conducted two case studies, Zambia and Mozambique, which represented the dominant trends in the continent, respectively weakly and highly institutionalised party systems that were at odds with democracy[3].

Since 2015, and as a research fellow, I have co-organized several editorial projects that somehow tapped into the functioning of democracy in Africa. Among other things, I have shown, together with colleagues, that even though elections have been held regularly in Africa, they have provoked only limited changes: the small group of countries that qualified as liberal democracies in the early 1990s has remained steady over the course of thirty years[4]. Currently, more than 80% of the 54 African countries feature elements of authoritarian rule to varying degrees (Freedom House, 2022). However, interestingly enough we also discovered that, if a country had experienced alternation in government in the founding multiparty elections this improved democratic performance and the odds of turnover in the future. The latter was also increased by the level of political competition

---

2 Sanches, E.R. (2014) *Explaining party system institutionalization in Africa: From a broad comparison to a focus on Mozambique and Zambia*. PhD Thesis. University of Lisbon (https://repositorio.ul.pt/bitstream/10451/15494/1/ulsd069288_td_Edalina_Sanches.pdf)

3 This research originated a book, including more countries and an extended period of time - Sanches, E.R. (2018) *Party Systems in Young Democracies: Varieties of institutionalisation in Sub-Saharan Africa*. London and New York: Routledge

4 These include countries such as Botswana, Mauritius, Cabo Verde, South Africa, Namibia, Ghana, São Tomé and Príncipe, and more recently Seychelles. Mali, Senegal and Benin were also part of this group but downgraded in the last decade. For more see Sanches, E.R, Macuane, J.J. & Dendere, C. (2019 "Introduction: Three decades of elections in Africa: what have we learned about democracy?" *Caderno de Estudos Africanos* 38, pp. 9-13.

and the quality of elections[5]. More recently, a book I edited
with Routledge draws on several country case studies to
demonstrate the relevant role of popular protest as engines
of change and democracy in Africa[6]. Indeed, not only they
have put democracy and good governance in the agenda, but
they also helped block presidents who attempted to change
the constitution to endure in power and scored significant
gains in terms of policy implementation and political rights[7].

Over the course of these years, I engaged with scholarly work
that, moving beyond the pessimistic narratives about the
state of democracy in Africa[8], questioned the western-based
liberal model of democracy and its imposition over the Global
South. Scholars such as Claude Ake, Kwasi Wiredu, or Reginald
Oduor, among many, make the case that this model is inimical
to African countries' cultural settings and communitarian
outlook. Instead, they propose the need to adapt democracy,
its principles and institutions, to the specific contexts within
which it operates. Crucially, they have proposed an African
model of democracy, based on consensual mechanisms to
mediate conflict and the views of different ethnolinguistic
groups, increased decentralisation and more direct forms of
democracy at the local level. Engaging with these scholars,
and social activists, has allowed me to discover new arenas
for democratic improvement and reinvention in Africa.

---

5 Sanches, E.R. & Macuane, J.J. "Elections as vehicles for change? Explaining
different outcomes of democratic performance and government alternation in
Africa." *Caderno de Estudos Africanos* 38, pp. 15-40.

6 Sanches, E.R. (Ed.) (2022) *Popular Protest, Political Opportunities and Changes in
Africa*. London: Routledge.

7 "'African presidents extending terms: 'Let's express our disapproval loud and
clear'" https://www.theafricareport.com/40199/african-president-extending-terms-
lets-express-our-disapproval-loud-and-clear/ (Accessed: 16-06-2022)

8 Particularly the views that highlight clientelism, weak and predatory states,
and presidentialism, among others, as the key sources of democratic failure
in Africa; while neglecting the long-term impacts of colonialism and its
contemporary repercussions.

For those beginning to study democracy, I strongly encourage you to look at third-wave countries, particularly Africa. They challenge some of the established theories about how democracies emerge and sustain over time (e.g. modernisation, social structure, type of political institutions and political culture theories). The field of studies on democratisation in Africa has expanded greatly in the past years, and there are countless interesting books from where to start. Here are some (selected) recommendations for a beginner in the topic: *Democratic Experiments in Africa* (Michael Bratton and Nicolas van de Walle); *Democracy and development in Africa* (Claude Ake); *Democracy in Africa: Successes, Failures, and the Struggle for Political Reform* (Nic Cheeseman); *Electoral Politics in Africa Since 1990: Continuity in Change* (Jaimie Bleck and Nicolas van de Walle); *Liberal Democracy and Its Critics in Africa: Political Dysfunction and the Struggle for Social Progress* (Tukumbi Lumumba-Kasonga); *Institutions and Democracy in Africa* (Nic Cheeseman); *Authoritarian Origins of Democratic Party Systems in Africa* (Rachel Beatty Riedl); *Africa's Media, Democracy and the Politics of Belonging* (Francis B. Nyamnjoh); *Digital Democracy, Analogue Politics: How the Internet Era is Transforming Politics in Kenya* (Nanjala Nyabola), among many others.

Democracy is not perfect, or the end of history, but rather an open-ended process where progressive and backward forces clash from time to time. It must be protected (e.g., by citizens, politicians and institutions), but more importantly it must be reinvented, to better address the challenges it faces across space and time (e.g., disenchantment, distrust, illiberalism, misfit, exit). I hope this short testimony inspires the reader to study democracy across its multiple arenas, country and time variations. I hope it also inspires her to help transform it.

(3) The Dark Side of Democracy

Luca Manucci

luca.manucci@ics.ulisboa.pt

I must confess this: I did not end up studying democracy on purpose. Let's say, it's something that 'happened' to me. In fact, after almost ten years, I would say that I do not really care about studying democracy. How did this happen, you ask? Let's start from the beginning.

I was living in the Netherlands, in Rotterdam to be precise, with a master's degree in *mass media and politics* in my pocket, while surviving thanks to the very cheap *lahmacun* from the Turkish restaurant next door. After a short – and admittedly unsuccessful – stint as a barista, I needed a job. I applied for a PhD position in Switzerland, and (to my bewilderment) it worked.

I moved to St. Gallen, a small and boring Swiss city near the Austrian border, and started my new life. This specific PhD position made me work for a project about political and media populism in Western Europe, which I thought was a cool way to combine my skills on media studies and political communication. Bingo! I thought. I was excited about the idea of studying populism because I am fascinated by the cringe, Schadenfreude-ish and pop-culture-related aspects of politics: the terrible haircuts of Trump, Wilders, and Berlusconi, the way in which Beppe Grillo was promising to revolutionise Italian democracy through online voting, the nefarious consequences of the economic crisis and the potential for social movements to seriously question

capitalism, Varoufakis vs. the Troika, the Tea Party and
Occupy Wall Street, the dog in a burning room saying "this
is fine," the alt-right kidnapping of Pepe the Frog…

I ended up studying none of those things, instead realising
that in fact I was enrolled in a PhD program on democracy
studies. I found myself dealing with things like data
collection, codebooks, methods, hypotheses, forming the
coders, doing analysis, presenting results…What I found
interesting, fascinating, and stimulating became cold
and repetitive. In other words: it became a job. Nothing
bad about that, especially if that job is very well paid,
your supervisor does not make your life impossible, your
colleagues are cool people, you have time to travel and
relax, you almost never feel inadequate or filled with
anxiety…what I'm trying to say is that, if the conditions
are right, doing a PhD in democracy studies is not bad.

You still wake up sweating in the middle of the night thinking
how to change a word in a chapter of your dissertation, or
with the sinister and foreboding feeling that you remember
a missing bibliographic reference from your literature
review, you still spend a couple of night and weekends
fixing problems and meeting deadlines, but after all it's a
totally acceptable job if done under favourable conditions.
Unfortunately, PhD students often experience discrimination,
sexism, racism, emotional blackmailing, insufficient pay,
stress, hostile supervisors, impostor syndrome, and mental
health problems. What for me has been a nice experience,
among other things thanks to my white male privilege, ends
up being a traumatic experience for many other people.

Ok, I am digressing. Surely there is enough of this in the section about doing a PhD, so let's go back on topic: democracy. I did not plan to study democracy and I did not have any particular interest in the topic. Very simply, I got hired for a project on populism, and only later I realized that I was enrolled in a PhD program on democracy studies. It turned out fine, but I still do not particularly care about 'democracy' as a topic of research. I am more interested in politics as a way to manage the common good, reduce inequalities, and plan out the future, but you don't need to study democracy to do these things. Actually, most politicians have a degree in law, or economy, and to be an activist all you have to do is to roll up your sleeves and try to improve the society where you live. You don't need abstracts, word limits, or citation styles.

Anyway, almost a decade after embarking on this path, I can say that what really interests me is the dark side of democracy: populism. Populism, for me, is not the opposite of democracy (that would be authoritarianism, dictatorship, or fascism). In Star Wars, the dark side of the force is defined as anger, fear, aggression, and a lust for power. Populism is essentially democratic, because it promises to give power to the people, and democracy literally means "the rule of the people". At the same time, populism is also the dark side of democracy because it is a vision of society where pluralism, separation of powers, minority rights, and media freedom are overshadowed by the charismatic leader who promises to embody the popular will. Populism is something that can be used for the best of purposes but might also have catastrophic consequences if used in the wrong way. Like nuclear energy, for example. Or the force.

Winston Churchill fought to preserve democracy against
the barbarism of Nazi-fascism. He also said, however,
that the best argument against democracy is a five-minute
conversation with the average voter. Without that average
voter, democracy would not exist, and populism places all
its legitimacy in the hands of *Joe the Plumber* and *Zé Povinho*.
At the same time, the will of the people is not a tangible
thing that can be condensed, put in a USB stick, and stuck
into a machine to produce laws that we all agree upon. The
volonté générale can only be expressed through a conflictual
process, often a bloody business, because different parts
of society have different interests, and in real life thesis-
antithesis-synthesis come only at great cost, through a huge
deal of conflict. This is what populism refuses to accept,
and why instead of fixing democracy it risks ruining it.

I like doing research on populism because it's dirty business.
I am particularly interested in democracy's malfunctions,
the threats and dangers that make democracy so fragile,
and populism is one of them. What fascinates me is the
fact that in Europe we experienced the folly of fascism and
Nazism, the concentration camps and the Shoah, racism
and discrimination, then we promised 'never again' and
yet, here we are. We're incredibly fascinated by strong,
charismatic leaders with dubious democratic credentials,
we follow whoever promises to be neither left nor right but
just against corruption, love easy promises and twitter-
friendly-revolutionaries, profess our love for democracy
but cannot tolerate opinion different from ours.

If in the attempt to protect the public discourse and democracy
from racism and fascism you draw a line between what can
be said and what cannot be said, some will tell you that you're

censoring them, so basically you become the undemocratic one who wants to limit freedom of speech. Cancel culture, the dictatorship of political correctness, and so on, you heard of it. Karl Popper already offered a valid argument against tolerating fascists. He said that "an open society needs to be intolerant of intolerance", therefore if you seek votes based on the facts that you want to expel migrants, imprison women who wear burkas, and silence the media you don't like, our society does not have a place for you, we won't tolerate you. This sounds like a paradox? Well, it should, because it is a paradox. Democracy is a mess, a constant tension between a pure, otherworldly ideal and our muddy, bloody, weird reality.

Now, to study democracy is way less exciting than it sounds like. On the other hand, being involved in associations, groups, activism and so on might be funny, interesting, and fulfilling. Studying democracy from the stuffy rooms of the ivory tower that is academia is another thing. For this reason, as soon as I started my PhD I realised that I needed a relief valve, a way to remain in contact with the weird, paradoxical, unsettling, and semiotically disturbing elements of society in general, and politics in particular. The gaffes of famous politicians, the promise to build a wall between the US and Mexico, Boris Johnson (like, the whole person), Greta Thunberg's braids, the Pizzagate and the fake allegations that Hillary Clinton was sexually abusing children in satanic rituals...well, you got the point. I needed an outlet for the cool, creepy, scary, funny stuff out there that cannot be included in academic papers, chapters, and books. Because even if some of it can actually be considered as academic material, the academic cycle of production simply cannot keep up with the rhythm of society. If something happens today, what's the point in waiting two and a half years, go through endless revisions, and doubt my self-worth, to publish an academic article about something that in the meantime is outdated?

For this reason, I decided to open a blog. In 2015 I created populismobserver.com where I publish articles and interviews on populism. This allowed me to have a space where I can store the weirdness, the uncanny, the unclassifiable, the pop aspects of politics, the partisan aspects of democracy, standing for a side, promoting an idea, expressing an opinion, instead of just pretending that we are impartial, equidistant, unbiased, god-like saviours who just stick to the *p-value*, believe nothing else but data, never venture into expressing an opinion because you never know whose feet you will step on. And now, seven years later, some of the interviews I published over time in my blog, together with other interviews realised specifically for this project, will be published by Routledge as a book: *The Populism Interviews*. So, maybe, researching democracy can be fun after all. But it's on you to make it happen.

(4) Political Participation and Direct Democracy

Arndt Leininger
arndt.leininger@phil.tu-chemnitz.de

I began to study political science for much of the same reasons that I think most of my students nowadays begin to study political science. I was motivated by a strong interest in politics and a desire to change certain things about the world, which led me to conclude that it might be useful to study political science. I was very interested in politics in my youth and actively involved in various causes. The topics that moved me at the time were, among others, the EU constitutional treaty, which ultimately failed because the French public rejected it in a referendum, early national elections in Germany in 2005 after the then ruling social democrats lost a state election in my home state North-Rhine Westphalia and the 2007 G8[1] summit in Heiligendamm, Germany.

Little did I know back then what the scientific study of politics entails. Neither did I anticipate that studying political science would mean learning about statistics, much less that I would actually end up liking that part in particular. Having evaded mathematics in high school as much as possible, it came somewhat as a surprise to me that I would come to do quantitative political science research for a living. While I remained politically active during my undergraduate studies, my intellectual interest in politics very strongly shifted toward a scientific study of politics. What interested me most was the question of whether there are any, if not

---

1 Precursor to the G7, which the G8 turned into after Russia was excluded from the group following its annexation of Crimea, Ukraine.

laws, empirical regularities in the area of elections and party competition. In short, I became interested in testing political science theories through quantitative data analysis.

Consequently, I pursued a strongly research-oriented masters at the London School of Economics. Of course, I was attracted by the academic program of this prestigious school but also the lure of a city that promised to be even more cosmopolitan than Berlin. It was an intense year – British master's programs often consist of a single year of study –, which I fondly remember for the many things I learned, and the friends I made, some of whom would later become co-authors. While preparing for the final exams, I applied to various Ph.D. programs. It turns out that many of these deadlines appear to be inconveniently timed. If you want to continue with a Ph.D. right after your master's, chances are you have to start applying before you even submit your master's thesis. Keep this in mind if you are a student reading this. Fortunately, one of my many applications was accepted, and I became part of the first cohort of the Hertie School's new Ph.D. program.

So I returned to Berlin, where the Hertie School, a private public-policy school and the first private university to receive the right to grant PhDs in Germany, is located. In the first year of my Ph.D., I worked in an MP's office in the German Bundestag to finance my studies. I quit the job after a year because I received a doctoral scholarship and wanted to focus entirely on my research. Nevertheless, during this brief spell in professional politics, I did learn a lot. Perhaps most importantly, at least for my current occupation as an academic researcher, I took with me the cautionary reminder that politics in practice is usually more complex than our elegant political science theories would often suggest.

Speaking of theory, as the editors of this book have asked us to define what democracy means to us, I would like to start with one of my favorite definitions. It was coined by Robert A. Dahl in his seminal book "Democracy and its critics,"[2] where he describes democracy as "an orderly and peaceful process by means of which a majority of citizens can induce the government to do what they most want it to do and to avoid doing what they most want it not to do." Of course, this is not all there is to modern democracies, which are best defined as liberal democracies. The term democracy implies that decisions are taken by majority rule, but the prefix liberal indicates that majorities are curtailed in what they can do when the rights of individuals or minorities are concerned. With this definition in mind, the study of democracy can be many things. One can study how countries become democracies but also, and there has been an increased focus on this question recently, how they fail. But most of the literature, and this is what I am most interested in, is concerned with how democratic systems make sure that government action is broadly in line with the preferences of the population.

In my research, I focus primarily on established democracies, especially my home country, Germany. Having grown up in one of the most advanced democracies, one might see studying the familiar as a sign of intellectual convenience. On the other hand, at least that is how I like to see it, one can interpret it as not taking the democratic freedoms that one grew up with for granted. When I began to study political science, electoral turnout was at an all-time low in Germany and many other countries after a decades-long secular decline. Turnout rates have since recovered somewhat but

2 Dahl, Robert Alan. *Democracy and Its Critics*. Yale University Press, 1989.

are still nowhere near where they used to be in the 1970s. This is puzzling because, since that time, wealth and education levels – all strong predictors of electoral participation at the individual level – have risen in basically all established democracies. This puzzle of declining turnout despite or (maybe because of?) continuous improvements in democracy and living standards represents a longstanding research interest of mine. Hence, one of my main research topics is what institutional reforms can increase voter turnout and whether and what impact that has on electoral outcomes.

At the same time, there have been discussions for many years in established democracies on how to give citizens a greater say in politics, be it on the local or the national level. Hence, another question that interests me is how democracy can be further developed. Here, direct democracy, allowing citizens to vote on substantive issues that parliamentarians usually deliberate and vote on, has an intuitive appeal to be the most apparent institutionalization of democracy itself. It is also arguably the most far-reaching and most popular reform proposed to provide a deepening and improvement of representative democracy.[3] I am interested in why this far-reaching but also quite demanding form of citizen participation is so popular. Another question that interests me is: Can citizens cope with the informational demands of the referendum, and how do they do so? As direct democracy is on the rise internationally – as evidenced by increased institutionalization and usage in many countries – this research topic might gain prominence in the years to come. In this and other research

<hr>

3 Leininger, Arndt. "Direct Democracy in Europe: Potentials and Pitfalls." *Global Policy* 6, Nr. S1 (2015): 17–27. https://doi.org/10.1111/1758-5899.12224.

areas, my aim is to pursue parsimonious theoretical explanations backed by rigorous empirical analysis.

That ideal is, I think, very well epitomized by the article "Electoral institutions and the politics of coalitions: Why some democracies redistribute more than others" by political scientists Torben Iversen and David Soskice, published in 2006 in the American Political Science Review.[4] I make this literature recommendation not because it makes a particularly crucial theoretical or empirical contribution to the study of democracy but rather because of how the authors approach their research question.

The authors' research question, as the paper's title suggests, is as follows: Why do some countries redistribute more than others? To answer this question, Iversen and Soskice develop a simple but elegant model of party competition, derive observable implications, and test these on data on electoral systems, government partisanship, and redistribution that they collected. Do not be put off by the mathematical jargon; you actually need to know next to nothing about formal modeling to be able to follow their argument. Both theoretical and empirical models are abstract and parsimonious and, hence, leave out many details, but that is precisely the point. Alas, I forgot where I read it, but I recall reading a textbook text as a student that likened theories to maps. Just like a good map leaves out most of the details of the area it covers to help you navigate it, a good model, theoretical or empirical, focuses on the important bits and leaves out the irrelevant. Of course, finding out what is important and what is not is part of that long and sometimes arduous scientific process. But when

---

4 Iversen, Torben, und David Soskice. "Electoral institutions and the politics of coalitions: Why some democracies redistribute more than others." *American Political Science Review* 100, Nr. 2 (2006): 165–181.

you manage to find such a theory, and it holds up to empirical scrutiny, you will find it is well worth the effort, I hope.

(5) A Democratic Ethos for Democracy Research

Hans Asenbaum
hans.asenbaum@canberra.edu.au

I always had a strong sense of social justice. In school, I was known for defending less popular kids and standing up to bullies. When I started studying political science at the University of Vienna, I was looking for a "political home." Although I engaged with subjects such as the political economy or the social state, it wasn't until I came across radical democratic thinking that I felt like I had arrived.

Strangely, it took a long time for me to realize the deep gap between these radical democratic convictions and the academic structures and practices within which I studied them. In other words, I was taught about equality in the midst of hierarchy. Academia appears as an exclusive black box, who admits only a select group of people, which first must pass a series of gatekeepers. Academia works according to neoliberal capitalist principles which stage an increasingly gamified competition between researchers. The system disciplines its participants into thinking and acting in a particular way. As a result, the knowledge produced through academia is rather uniform.

We spend all day reading and writing about a democratic ethos that promotes equality, inclusion, and transparency within an exclusive, competitive, and hierarchal environment. In this chapter, I will engage with this contradiction. In doing so, I will attempt to bring three aspects together. I will, first, tell my own story of my academic development and share some personal confessions. Second, in sharing these insights, I will generate helpful tips for PhD and Early Career Researchers. Third, I will provide a critique of the current undemocratic workings of academia and moreover, share some thoughts on how to move beyond them by incorporating a democratic ethos into democracy research.

Democratic ideals within an undemocratic context
When I started my PhD in Vienna, I was excited. For the first time in several years of studies, I felt recognized and appreciated. I attended seminars and group meetings and finally mustered the courage to speak up – a courage I was lacking throughout most of my undergrad and grad studies. I went to conferences and started to publish. Everybody in my research group was friendly and driven by similar progressive convictions that I held dear myself. These qualities easily mask the exclusions that are deeply embedded in the structures of modern-day academia, which mirror the power asymmetries of their capitalist, heteropatriarchal, and colonial context. I hardly realized how privileged I was to join the inner academic circle. I did not reflect on the societal privileges in my biography that had led me here.

Despite the friendly welcome, academia felt like a murky ground. I wasn't quite sure what I was doing and how this whole thing actually works. I am still confronted with this puzzlement today when I talk to others outside academia about my job. "I'm a political scientist." "Oh, so you are a politician? Or one of these TV guys that talk about elections? Ah, you're a teacher at uni." The confusion about what political scientists do – my mum doesn't really understand what I'm doing to this day – speaks of a certain exclusivity. Academia presents itself as a black box. Its opaqueness, I reckon, is no coincidence. Those in privileged positions have several motives to shield what they are doing from public scrutiny. For once, shrouding the workings of academia keeps competition out. It requires friends, connections – the (in)famous "network" – to slowly learn to navigate academia. One needs to convince gatekeepers to open the doors.

So if you are new to all this, first of all, confusion is normal. How do conferences work? What is the H-Index? Do I need to wait for a call for papers to submit a paper to a journal? Do I get paid for research visits at another unis? It might be consoling that to most of these questions, there is no fixed answer – answer vary depending on context and on whom you ask. So, ask many people. Don't be afraid to look naïve. I talked to lots of people who were more advanced in their careers. Just drop them an email, they will mostly be happy to chat. Moreover, peer support is crucial. I had a wonderful PhD community at the University of Westminster, in which we talked about the curiosities of academic life over lunch every day.

Upon entering the black box, one of the first things you will learn is that publishing is key. Publishing is a highly exclusive business, in which the academic institutional system shapes what you can say and how you can say it. Ultimately, academia shapes who you are. Do Foucault's disciplinary institutions come to mind? Yes, that's what it is. Publishing is only partly merit-based. In many ways, the current system discourages from being original and innovative. Reviewers can easily take issue with anything you say. As a result, writing can sometimes feel like walking on egg shells. "What could reviewers dislike? On whose toes might I step? How can I reframe this in a less controversial way?" Writing can easily turn into an exercise of avoiding mistakes. At the same, novelty and originality are key criteria for publishing. Sounds contradictory? It is. So what we often end up doing is while walking on eggshells making big gestures with our hands. It's like dancing only with your upper body without moving the lower half of your body. You need to "sell your message big" while the message itself needs to be as uncontroversial as possible. Of course, I'm being a bit polemic here. But you get the idea.

This is not to say that we cannot say anything politically meaningful through academic publications. Mostly, however, our texts are kept behind paywalls and guarded by steep access fees. Only those with university affiliations and those willing to pay will have access. This is ironic in the face of the fact that social science research is mostly funded through public tax money. The public has a right to access this knowledge. Research is part of public discourse. It does not make sense to keep ideas, which are meant to benefit society, within what is often referred to the "academic ivory tower."

Towards a democratic ethos
This all sounds very bleak. So what can we do about it? On my journey through the obscurities of academic life, I have met many inspiring people who have opened new perspectives for me. They showed me that it is not always necessary to succumb to academic pressures. They aim at realizing a democratic ethos within a context that is not particularly welcoming.

A good starting point to do things differently is teaching. Often, we begin teaching as PhD candidates when we are still struggling with our own insecurities (not that this struggle ever ends, but it gets better). Applying various teaching methods that require different skills can include students with various talents. Learning can not only be achieved by reading books but by going out there and engaging in first-hand research and political projects. Many aspects of teaching, such as reading lists and grading criteria, can be decided collectively with students. We need to profoundly rethink our relationship with students and move away from a hierarchical student-professor and towards a peer-mentoring relationship.

Realizing a democratic ethos in the actual research process can take many forms. This can be achieved through participatory research methods that invite participants into the research project to collaboratively decide its parameters and generate and analyse data. Crucially, a democratic ethos will steer us towards research topics that shed light on marginalized groups, discourses, and phenomena. Being not only democracy researchers but democratic researchers entails playing an active role in society, for example by setting up participatory processes or collaboratively developing them with social movements and civil society actors. I try to realize a democratic ethos in my own research. I developed a new method for generating democratic theory, which I call *democratic theorizing*. I set up the Democratic Theorizing Project[1], which invites anyone into a joint theorizing process.

Importantly, realizing a democratic ethos in democracy studies entails self-reflection and a critical engagement with our own positionality. Where do we stand? Which privileges do we hold? Which interests do we and others have? Which impact does our research have? Such self-reflective processes feeds into a deconstructive approach that challenges the colonial, capitalist, and heteropatriarchal structures that govern our academic engagements.

---

1 https://democratic-theorizing.org/

When it comes to research output, making academic
knowledge accessible to the public is crucial. This includes
making an effort in open access publishing. This may entail
looking for resources to cover open access fees. But it also
includes supporting smaller open access journals and
presses such as The Journal of Deliberative Democracy,
Democratic Theory, and Westminster University Press.
But open publishing goes beyond open access. It entails
writing in an accessible manner. This does not preclude
a high level of abstraction or a deep engagement with
philosophical work. It may entail writing for different
audiences in different styles, translating abstract
ideas into more concrete terms, and communicating
via various academic and non-academic outlets.

In the face of the criticism I have raised, the question arises
whether one should play this game at all. It is a personal choice
whether one decides to work on changing the rules of the game
or quitting the game altogether. For me personally, despite all
its hierarchical and exclusive aspects, academia still provides
a space for public debate, a means to develop critical and
alternative thinking that challenges the mainstream. Driven
by a democratic ethos, democracy research can play a vital
role in societal transformations toward democratic futures.

Literature tip: Ackerly, B., Cabrera, L., Forman, F., Johnson,
G. F., Tenove, C., & Wiener, A. (2021). Unearthing Grounded
Normative Theory: Practices and Commitments of Empirical
Research in Political Theory. *Critical Review of International
Social and Political Philosophy, 0*(0), 1–27. https://doi.org/10.1080/
13698230.2021.1894020

(6) Personal Confession on the Study of Democracy

Su Yun Woo
woo@ipz.uzh.ch

The path to democracy studies is paved with good intentions

So, no one told me that studying/pursuing a PhD in Democracy Studies would be this way – fascinating, frustrating, and ultimately very fruitful. If I were to be honest, I did not expect myself to do a PhD, let alone one on democracy. As someone who was born and raised in Singapore, a country whose democratic credentials are rather weak, at least in the Western liberal democratic sense, democracy has always been an idea(l) that seemed abstract and ambivalent. Even when I studied the concept in the political science classes during my undergraduate days, it always felt foreign. Sure, I had taken courses on political theory that encompasses democratic ideas, and even the more in-depth engagement with democracy during my Masters studies at ETH Zurich, Switzerland did provoke some reflection. However, to me, democracy belonged to the pages of the textbooks and maybe news reports that highlight the triumphs, and now trials, of democracy. Interestingly enough, the Singaporean national pledge (which every student has to recite faithfully for at least a good 10 years of their school life) does include a line about "to build a democratic society," although years of being uttering this line still made me rather indifferent to democracy. Simply put, my emotional detachment from democracy stems from my lack of lived experience with democracy. Accustomed to the highly efficient and depoliticized Singaporean society,

I was apathetic and democracy was such a distant idea
and ideal that seemed absent from my everyday life.

In an odd turn of events, when I was contemplating quitting
a highly stressful job in a start-up and mulling over an
alternative career, the opportunity to pursue a PhD in
democracy studies came up. In an even odder turn of events,
the eventual focus for this PhD would be on China, and thus
began my fortuitous adventure with democracy, albeit with
Chinese characteristics. As if this was not already challenging
enough, I decided to adopt the deliberative democratic lens
to study China. Serendipity perhaps? Or you could say that
the topic of deliberative democracy in China kind of fell onto
my lap. And this was more of a *Bildungsroman* than a fairy
tale. What seemed like a typical pursuit of academic inquiry
became so much more as I, if you would allow me to put it
rather tritely, found my (democratic) self. Researching about
Chinese democracy, an anomaly that sits uncomfortably
with many, in Switzerland, a deeply democratic country, was
and is still no walk in the park. Not only did I have to revisit
the democratic debates, especially the ones relating to the
deliberative democratic literature, which is one deeply rooted
in political theory that can be convoluted and confounding to
me, I also had to grapple the Chinese democratic discourses
which were equally, if not more convoluted and confounding.
While I was wrestling with the academic anxieties of having
to make sense of the complexities in navigating this research
topic, it did not help that I had encountered lots of skepticism
whenever I mentioned both democracy and China in the same
sentence. Over time, I became used to the looks of disbelief
and slight smirk of doubt as I calmly try to convince my
audience of the democratic possibilities that do exist in China.

Is democracy in China a unicorn?

And yes, democracy in China is not a unicorn! It does exist, although there are many caveats and clarifications that I can only try to shed some insights without regurgitating the 250 pages of my PhD dissertation. How do I start to peel off the layers of meanings and explanations regarding this (like an onion), without starting to cry from the sheer difficultly of it? As a disclaimer, I do not seek to espouse a Chinese model of democracy that glosses over the undemocratic elements of the system. Rather, as a useful starting point, I just wanted to provide some thought-provoking opportunities by highlighting the presence of democratic experiments and democratic possibilities. Now I can imagine that the immediate reaction emanating from the West is surely one of denial and denouncement, especially since this vision and version of Chinese democracy runs contrary to their assessment of the situation in China. However, I think that controversy creates the opportunity for reflection as it will be more constructive to scrutinize the contents of the functioning form of Chinese democracy and to ponder about the intention and implications of this discourse.

But it is difficult to move beyond the polarized and binary perspective of democratic development in China. I often struggle with the challenge of examining China's democratic processes since they are often viewed as a window dressing that justifies the authoritarian rule of the Chinese Communist Party, and thus is a total inappropriate appropriation of Western ideals. The truth, as banal and unsatisfactory as it may sound, lies in the grey area of "it is and it is not." While yes, there is a broader political system that is clearly undemocratic in the eyes of the West, but there are other levels of politics, for example the local level, where democratic experiments have proliferated. I had the chance to study local deliberative processes for my PhD research project and benefited tremendously from the fieldwork conducted in China where I was able to observe the processes and interview the stakeholders. This was a formative experience that allowed me to broaden my intellectual horizon and challenge me to engage with a democratic discourse that is articulated rather differently from the Western canon. What I further appreciated was the opportunity to reflect about the local definition and development of deliberative democracy, one that is localized and adapted to the local conditions and requires the unorthodox reconciliation with a broader non-democratic context. I am honest enough to confess that the contradictions and complexities in China continue to befuddle me and compel me to not only persist in the pursuit of this topic, but also to challenge me to step out of the comfort zone of envisioning a different trajectory of democracy.

There is a lot to talk about when we talk about Chinese democracy, or democracy with Chinese characteristics, a loaded and provocative way of framing and understanding democratic development in China. In my own research, I tried to situate the emergence of deliberative practices within the democratic development of China and found that there is a plurality and diversity in democratic innovations in different Chinese localities. On the one hand, the more developed and affluent East Coast province of Zhejiang adopted a form of democratic deliberation through the institutionalization of a Participatory Budgeting (PB) process that follows somewhat the Western model. On the other hand, Chengdu, a city in the less affluent and developed Southwestern part of China, has localized and improvised upon a model of PB that has democratic potential of empowering citizens to

participate in local governance. Chengdu has even taken
a step further to innovate on its local PB innovation, by
bringing PB to social media (WeChat[1], which is akin to
WhatsApp but with many more functionalities) in an attempt
to enhance the equality of participatory opportunities
and policy transparency. As always, I am clear eyed about
the motivations of these democratic experiments given
that the ultimate goal is to strengthen the one-party rule
and not so much about realizing normative goals. The
democratic quality of some of these processes and the
democratic promise, however, can still be rather credible.

Small d instead of big D

Speaking about democracy in China may be provocative
but it allows an entry point to reflect about the many facets
of democracy and the disputes over these can actually
democratize our understanding of democracy. Instead of
promulgating the big D, more about a democratic model
usually based on the Western liberal representative model,
we can think about the small d, where democracies can take
on different forms. In fact, scholars have started to engage
with such a possibility, exploring the anomaly of non-Western
democracies[2], at the same time challenging the monopolistic
understanding of democracy, which is one heavily centered
on the histories, philosophies and experiences of the West.
This approach also responds to the burgeoning calls to
decolonize the study of democracy, so delving into the
intricacies of democracy with Chinese characteristics clearly
contributes to the expansion of the democratic discourse.

---

1 In a pretty blatant and shameless plug, I would share this short piece that I
have written to shed some insights on this. https://deliberativehub.wordpress.
com/2021/07/26/participation-with-chinese-characteristics-wechat-participatory-
budgeting-in-chengdu/

2 Youngs, R. (2015). The Puzzle of non-western democracy. Brookings Institution Press.

Using the Chinese democratic lens to ponder about the study
of democracy in a broader sense no doubt risks undermining
the universal qualities that democracy possesses. This is
an often-heard argument that is not without its merits, but
who decides on the set of universal features underpinning
democracy? And the ability to shape and establish this
democratic standard lies ultimately in the West, and
alternative conceptions of democracy remained marginalized.

Even non-Western countries like China espouse a people-
centric approach to governance, an idea that empowers the
demos which is a crucial fundamental principle of democracy.
It is however not easy for the Chinese democratic discourse
to be recognized by the West, mainly because of the uneasy
and contradictory co-existence of democratic features with an
authoritarian one-party state. Yet while the procedural forms
of democracy in the form of electoral democracy and universal
suffrage are missing in China, there are high levels of
governmental performance and citizens' satisfaction. Perhaps
democracy in China is indeed more about the performance
aspect, as suggested in a recent white paper[3] that the Chinese
government published. It heralds a "democracy that works,"
a subtle jab at the Western model whose malfunction
has become a topic of concern with the current mood of
democratic backsliding. What does this mean then, not only
for the unique form of Chinese democracy, but more for the
field of democratic studies, to assess democracy more in terms
of its output? We already have many indicators measuring
democracy, so this focus on output is not so revolutionary
after all. But the more pertinent point to highlight here is
to consider how a disaggregated approach to democracy,
the small d, can be present in unusual places like China.

---

3 http://www.news.cn/english/2021-12/04/c_1310351231.htm

Free your mind of democratic dogma

In the end, I am not sure if I have the answer, or even answers, to the continuous conundrum of trying to study the complicated and complex world of democracy, or should I rather say democracies. I sometimes wished that someone could have waved the red flag to me before I dived into the deep blue sea to try and navigate the intriguing waters of democracy studies. Although I have to admit, this has still been a worthwhile journey to undertake. Not knowing what to expect can also allow one to free the mind of dogmatic thinking. To me, this is probably a deep-seated conviction I have come to acquire over the course of trying to make sense of the Chinese democratic discourse, an endeavor I continue to pursue, with the wide-eyed optimism that someday I might just get to the light at the end of the tunnel. Do I now have the benefit of hindsight to dispense one piece of advice? Maybe I do. It is important to free your mind of dogmatic democratic ideas, to challenge and deconstruct what democracy means, not so much to destroy but to defend what democracy can be, not so much what it is. At the risk of reiterating this sentiment *ad nauseum*, democracy is essentially a contested and ongoing project. This should not be deemed as frightening, but rather, we should feel excited about the confusion caused by the plurality and democratization of democracy studies to stretch and expand our academic imagination.

Part B

*

Being a PhD Researcher

This section is the longest of the book, with "confessions" from former and current PhD candidates. We asked the authors to tell us the story of their time as a PhD candidate – what was their PhD experience like? We have asked people with very different journeys. Some did quit their PhDs while others have thrived in it. Some have decided to remain in academia, others have moved on to different fields. Some authors have struggled with internal obstacles: anxieties, fears, self-doubts. Others with external obstacles: lack of funding, lack of support from institutions and supervisors, reconciling family and academic work. Some have found or created the right internal and external conditions to make for an enjoyable PhD experience. Many have wondered at some point of the journey what they were doing, and why. Most have found small and big victories along the way and learned more lessons than they ever thought they would. Here, they describe critical moments and crucial insights related to their personal experience. And most importantly, we asked everyone – if they could give one (and only one) advice to young PhD candidates – what would that advice be?

(7) In the Middle of a Storm it Feels Awfully Quiet

Lea Heyne
lea.heyne@ics.ulisboa.pt

I think that I have to preface this confession with another
confession: had I realized that co-editing a book on how to
survive a PhD would mean that apart from asking others to
do so, *I* would have to write about my own PhD experience
as well, I would probably have hesitated much more to
engage in this project. However, I'm very glad that we
did come through with this book project, and that my co-
editor Chris convinced me to write a contribution too!

I guess the reason that I was reluctant to write a confession
is that I honestly still don't like to think back at my time as
a PhD student, or at least, not at all aspects of it. Without
any doubt, many amazing things happened to me during
those 4 years, and I do consider myself very lucky for all
the fantastic opportunities that I had. But still, doing, and
especially finishing, a PhD was the most difficult and soul-
crushing thing I've ever experienced. In retrospective,
looking back at the last year or so of my PhD, it genuinely feels
like something that I survived, like a natural disaster. As if
somehow, and without even really realizing it, I ended up in
the center of a storm that I had to struggle hard to get out of.

But let's start from the beginning. I did my PhD in democracy
studies from 2013 to 2017, in a research project on democratic
quality that I was, at least initially, very passionate about.
I always liked university and had already worked as a
research assistant during my BA and my MA, professors had

encouraged me to pursue an academic career, and so doing a PhD seemed like the obvious choice. I was very excited when I got accepted for a position in Zurich, it seemed like a huge win: great university, great project, great funding opportunities. And it was a win, in so many ways: I met lots of interesting people, I had the chance to go to conferences in Europe and America, to learn from cool scholars that I had always admired. I found great peers and colleagues, and started working on projects that I loved, such as DemocracyNet. I felt like I had found my "place." For the first time in my life, I earned enough money to not worry about anything, and to travel. I finally managed to end a complicated relationship, and later fell in love with my current partner. Life was good, and I felt very lucky to be doing what I was doing.

At the same time, two things gradually worsened as I was approaching the end of my PhD. First of all, my self-doubts, anxiety, and imposter syndrome. The deeper I got into my PhD research, the more I felt like I knew absolutely nothing, like what I was doing didn't really matter at all. I know that many – probably almost all – PhD students struggle with similar issues, and while I often found it hard to cope with those feelings, I think I would have been able to deal with them as well (or unwell) as everyone else. But the second thing that deteriorated was the relationship with my supervisor (who was also the project leader), and clearly, this is what made things increasingly difficult for me. If someone gives you the feeling that you and what you are doing is wrong, that you don't work in the way you should, and that you can't count on their support, it certainly doesn't help with your self-doubts and anxiety. I remember that at some point I was so anxious about the situation that only receiving an email from my supervisor made me panic, and it took all my willpower to open and read it. I remember trying to train for conversations with my supervisor, with my therapist at the time (who I was seeing for completely different reasons, but who ended up mostly helping me with PhD related issues). I still often wonder what I could and should have done better to make this relationship less difficult, but the fact that many other peers who worked with me at the time experienced similar issues also made me realize that much of it was not my fault.

Apart from the support that I had from my partner, friends, colleagues, and my therapist, what probably protected me during the very difficult last months of my PhD was my healthy pragmatism and the fact that I always saw the PhD as a job, and had a good enjoyable life outside of this work, as well as my (probably less healthy) ability to ignore any problem if it seems too big to solve. Hence, what I did was simply working towards a very clear goal: Somehow finishing the PhD, getting away from my supervisor, and move on to the better things in life. And I did exactly that – I finished, although not without one last, terrible experience in the form of a pretty traumatic PhD defense, which until this day I can only remember in fragments.

Probably luckily for me, I had so many things to deal with right after the defense that I didn't have time to really reflect how bad this whole experience had been. I had already planned to take a long sabbatical with my partner, more than one year of traveling through Asia, so I immediately packed up all my things, left Switzerland, and embarked on a long and beautiful journey – probably the best year of my entire life. This trip saved me in more than one way. After my defense, I couldn't sleep, I wasn't hungry, I felt apathetic and very far away from everyone else. I was still in survival

mode. But as soon as I had my backpack on and got onto
the first train of many, things got better. And slowly, while I
was crossing the Iranian desert, the Pamir mountains, and
uncountable Chinese night markets, I could start unpacking
and processing all the feelings that I had bottled up during
the last months. I felt like I could breathe again, after a long
time of anxiously holding my breath, and of constantly
thinking something was going to go very, very wrong. I had
finally escaped that storm, and only when I had stepped out
of it I realized how terrifying it had actually been in there.

During and right after the trip, I was sure of one thing: I
was never, ever going to come back to academia. I felt like
academia had kicked me out and closed the door behind me,
and I was way too proud to come back and knock on it again.
But, as we all know, one should never say never – and when
I saw a postdoc position opening in 2019 that would allow
me to work in Lisbon, where my partner had just found a job
as well, I decided to give it one last chance. One application.
And to my own surprise, I got the job! So I stepped back into
doing research, this time luckily with a different experience.
First in a team with a supportive project leader, and recently
changing to a position where I now work independently
and have my own project. This has also allowed me to make
peace with academia, and to enjoy again the things that I
always loved about research: collaborating with interesting
people, getting to think and write and teach about the
topics that I care about, and enjoying the freedom that
comes from being able to work in my own time and pace.

So in retrospective, I don't regret having done a PhD, because
it has allowed me to live the good life that I live now, and to
work in a job that I genuinely like. And yet, I would never go

back to those moments in 2017 when I was trying to finish my
PhD, not for all the money in the world. I still have anxiety
each time that I open emails from people whose professional
opinions are important for me, scared that they will tell me
I'm wrong, or not enough – a reflection of my past experiences.
I still have nightmares in which my PhD is taken away from
me. I don't know if that will ever change, but I do know that
I will always try my best to create more healthy working
environments whenever I get the chance to do so. And I have
learned that even if I am resilient enough to deal with bad
experiences, one does not have to get through everything. You
can also step away, out of bad situations. In retrospective, I
should have done exactly that – I should at least have taken a
step back, looked at the bigger picture, and figured out what
is going wrong, and how it can be fixed. I guess that this is
also my advice to any potential or current PhD students:
to keep the big picture in mind, and not to get tricked into
thinking that living in the eye of a storm is necessary. It's
not. Yes, a PhD can be stressful at times, but it shouldn't
overwhelm you or make you feel anxious or depressed.

If something feels wrong, it probably is wrong, and rather
than biting your way through it, it's better to take a step back
and change it. A PhD is, after all, only a degree - it should
never take over your life.

(8) Money, Money, Money, must be Funded?

Chiara Valsangiacomo
chiara.valsangiacomo@uzh.ch

Pursuing an academic career was never on my radar as a child
or young adult. As a first-generation college student, I was
not even aware of the existence of doctoral degrees until well
into my master's degree. Back then, it struck me as surreal
that doing research in the humanities and social sciences
was the bread and butter of a significant number of people,
also known as scholars. When I finally did realize, around
spring 2017, that academia can be an employer like any other,
I knew this could be an interesting path for my future.

Fast forward one year, with my master's degree successfully
concluded, I was earning a good living as a research
assistant in Zurich. In the spare time, I was drafting my
project proposal for a PhD in political theory to further
my knowledge on the idea of liquid democracy. With this
research plan in my hands, I applied for several doctoral
programs across Europe, and reached out to potential
supervisors who all seemed enthusiastic about my project.
For some reasons, I assumed that securing the blessings
from professors together with a spot in a leading doctoral
program would come first, and this would automatically
guarantee a funded position. Little did I know, this is clearly
not how you raise money for your research and, by the time
I realized this, I had missed all deadlines for funding.

As all my plans were falling apart, I decided that the wisest
choice was to stay home, in Switzerland, where I could work

and have the support of my partner and family. In fall 2018,
I enrolled in a doctoral program at the University of Zurich,
without funding. My financial situation was far from ideal,
although it was not unheard of and, luckily, I was never flat
broke. For the next one and a half year, I was job hopping
from a teaching assistantship to yet another research
assistantship, and, after having signed up for unemployment
benefits, I temporarily left the university to work in a library
for aquatic science for four months. In the meanwhile, my
research was not really moving forward, and my curriculum
vitae was not shining bright with all these short-lived part-
time positions. Also, my first two funding applications were
rejected. Eventually, in spring 2020, I became the recipient
of a two-and-a-half-year scholarship issued by the Swiss
National Science Foundation. A happy ending at last.

As this story shows, plenty of things went adrift at the
beginning of my doctoral degree, some of which were totally
out of my control, while others depended at least partly on me.
I am sure that some readers might be interested in the lessons
I have learned first-hand from this personal experience. To
be fair, I am perfectly aware that all the anecdotes above will
hardly generalize to different countries, research disciplines,
personal histories, or attitudes. For example, working part-
time to finance your studies might not be a viable option if your
institution expects you to pay astronomical tuition fees. Also,
receiving a project grant will most likely force you to complete
your research within a certain time horizon that might not suit
you if you, for example, have care duties or medical conditions
that necessarily and understandably slow down your pace. Not
to mention that your thirst for knowledge might be such that
you consciously accept all these economic risks and decide
to go for it, against all odds. Without neglecting all these

caveats, my hope is that the following reflections will provide, if not guidance, at least some comfort to other (prospective) doctoral students who are navigating similar challenges.

The first lesson I have learned is that finding a supervisor and being accepted into a doctoral program is not the same as securing a salary. Indeed, finding someone who will pay for your research project is a different ball game, it is an art of its own, which requires some skills, preparation, and experience. I wish I had started gathering pieces of information earlier, even more so because there is plenty of preventive action one can take in this regard. So, do your homework: read a lot, and carefully, about the available options in your country. If needed, ask someone to introduce you to the local academic job market, and to elucidate for you the possible alternatives. Being an assistant for a chair where you must teach is different from being hired to collaborate within a broader research project, or from receiving a grant to carry out your own independent research. Do not disregard workshops on how to write grant proposals or coaching programs offered by universities, and, if your university does not offer such services or you do not have access to them, consider hiring a professional coach who is familiar with the funding institution you are targeting (yes, I have done this too). Keep in mind that, within academia, it is the rule to apply for funding about one year before the desired start of the project. Since writing a grant application can require months of nearly full-time dedication, the sooner you begin gathering information, the better.

No matter your efforts, sometimes starting a PhD without research funding might be the only alternative beside quitting at the very onset. This raises the proverbial question, to leave or not to leave? I truly believe that this is no easy choice, and, by the way, opting to stay is neither wrong nor impossible. If you are motivated to get that Dr. title, I am sure you will do it successfully and without regrets. That said, if you, like me, ended up pursuing (part of) your PhD without research funding and this was not your preferred plan, chances are you will be navigating some rough waters. Here is the second lesson I have learned: self-financing your PhD can be extremely stressful and frustrating, and you should be aware of this so that you can take the necessary precautions. While I did not expect it to be a fast buck, working next to the PhD was really challenging and it took a big toll on me. Just when I was getting used to the prospects of my adult life, with a good job and a decent salary, I plunged back into a miserable student life, with all the unpleasant feelings of uncertainty and vulnerability that come with it. Money, not my PhD, was my number one concern. Add to this a few other major challenges in my private life, plus the growing awareness that being an unfunded PhD student carries a certain stigma within the academic industry,[1] and the damage was done. I was constantly feeling nervous, overwhelmed, worried, envious, and marginalized. Life as an unfunded PhD student can be a real mental struggle, and I encourage you to take this risk very seriously into account.

As obvious as it sounds, self-financing your PhD is time-consuming, and this will impact the schedule of your project. The third lesson I have learned is that wearing many different hats requires organization and prioritization. Multitasking has its limits because—breaking news—there is only so much you can do with twenty-four hours a day, and, most of the

---

1 For another honest and relatable confession-like article about the widespread stigma around doing a PhD without research funding, see Natascha Chtena's "Unfunded Ph.D.s: To Go or Not To Go" (2013).

time, chasing hundreds of moving targets at once does not help. Despite all my efforts, my thesis was coming along with more difficulties and delays than I wished, and my brain was just not keeping up. I started second-guessing my choice of staying. So, when I received the first grant rejections in spring 2019, I had to redefine my priorities. The plan was to reduce the maintenance of my PhD to a minimum in order to channel all my energies into working and writing one more grant application for the September round. At that point, I had also identified my deal breaker: another rejection would have represented the last straw, and I was committed to peacefully leave if I did not get the money. In hindsight, I am glad I decided to slow down my research to focus primarily on grant writing. That break of several months allowed me to breathe and reset. Not surprisingly, once I got the funding, I caught up on everything I had left behind so quickly, and it was all downhill from there.

Finally, one more important lesson I have learned is that starting a PhD without research funding is more common than I expected. As a matter of fact, this seems to be a broader but often neglected problem in academia. Over the past four years, I have talked to a number of junior and senior scholars in the humanities and social sciences, many of whom have been unfunded researchers at some point in their careers. If it is true that a trouble shared is a trouble halved, by all means, do not isolate yourself and talk to people. Grab a coffee with other PhD students and colleagues and ask them if they are willing to talk about their own financial situation. Find a trusted friend, or a mentor, who can advise you and guide you throughout your journey. Mine is only one of countless stories. The more you will expose yourself to the experiences of other people, the larger the pool of possible ideas from which you will be able to

draw strategies to address your own issues. Being connected,
open-minded, and creative will help you keeping up the good
spirit you need to navigate the challenges of an unfunded PhD.

(9) Mountain Climber

Deborah Kalte
deborah.kalte@hotmail.com

Before I share with you my experience doing a PhD, I'd like to delve into this image I found scrolling through my Twitter feed one day. This picture instantly got my attention, stopped my scrolling, and started to stir quite some emotional turmoil inside of me. It made me go through these corner stones of my PhD, from preparing for my PhD interview until defending my thesis.

Source: PhScribble. https://twitter.com/PhScribble (posted on January 23, 2022). On a personal remark, I highly recommend following this account, as she posts refreshing and insightful experiences conducting her PhD.

The picture so aptly expresses how I feel when I think of my PhD: At the beginning, I had some idea about the subject I so excitedly wanted to spend the next couple of years on, and at the end, after having spent such a substantial part of my life studying this subject, I felt like I was merely holding a fraction of knowledge of it. More importantly though, the last sentence in this picture gets to the heart of what a PhD is about in my view: That I learned a lot about myself.

Let's start with the beginning of my PhD, a little bit before the PhD interview. After quitting my job in public administration, I felt going back to academia, as I missed researching and writing a lot. When I first saw the job advertisement for a research project on political consumerism, and that they were looking for a research assistant and PhD student, I had mixed feelings. I was immensely interested in this project, as it was set out to do empirical research on the consumer behavior of Swiss citizens and to study its political implications. But the prospect of doing a PhD felt like as if I would be climbing the Mount Everest. What an adventure, what a challenge this would be, the greatest I have ever done. I was excited. And I put all my efforts in this application and the interview. As I haven't studied this subject before in my Masters' or Bachelors' studies, I did a lot of research before the interview. I had a pretty decent understanding of the subject, but it was mainly my interest that I think convinced the project leaders to choose me. I was overjoyed and can still remember exactly where I was when I received the call to learn about their decision.

The project was already in its early stages when I joined the team. From the beginning, I could assist with the survey instrument, dive into the literature, and start developing my own PhD project within the larger project. It was an energizing time, and I enjoyed working on this subject every day. I had the fortune to work closely with the principal investigator, who guided me throughout the time. I was grateful to be able to discuss and find a way with her through the jungle of theories, findings, concepts, statistical analyses, and so on. And I was also very grateful for being in a PhD program with so many great people, who made going through that jungle much easier and sometimes even fun. As it is so nicely depicted in the cartoon above, the more I read and learned about the subject, the more I realized how vast it really is, and what I knew and what my PhD will add to it was really small. This feeling never really left me. However, I also came to realize that no matter how small my contribution to this field was, it nevertheless was a contribution. A small brick of a big building whose only purpose is to become solid, bigger and more colorful. And this is what doing a PhD is, to find your spot and proudly fill it out.

But there is another, and I think even more important task at hand when doing a PhD. Namely to learn more about yourself, which I definitely did. Particularly in the final months of my PhD, when all came down into writing one single, final piece of manuscript, I have learned where my limits are. Since this is a confession, I will be honest here. It was a very, very stressful and nerve-wrecking time. I was working almost every day plus weekends in the last few months before the final submission of the manuscript. And given that it was right during the Covid pandemic when several restrictions were in place, I did rarely go out to sports training class or meet friends. I felt like a hermit sometimes! I often feared, I would not make it in time or anyway, and I had to convince myself almost every day, that I could do it. But in the end, I did.

The day I defended my thesis is the day where all those
four years of my PhD came together. The nervousness,
the excitedness, and the sadness of this wonderful project
to end. And I was very happy to share this moment with
all my friends and colleagues that I have met along the
way. It was unfortunately an online defence because
of the Covid restrictions, but nonetheless, seeing so
many of my friends joining me online made these rather
stressful three hours a celebration! And this is, in my
view, is another great experience of doing a PhD, namely
to get to learn not only yourself but others who, just like
myself, are curious about learning more, exploring the
world and climbing one's personal Mount Everest.

(10) There's no Way in!? – How We Study Japanese Democracy from our German University

Stefanie Schwarte and Anne-Sophie L. König
s.schwarte@lmu.de
an.koenig@lmu.de

This is the confession of two third-year PhD students at the Japan Center LMU Munich, Germany. Coming from Japanese studies/area studies, venturing out into the field of democracy studies, we noticed that Japan, a liberal democracy since 1947 with a multiparty system under the dominance of the Liberal Democratic Party of Japan, is not usually at the top of everybody's head right away in regards to testing democratic theory. When we started studying Japan for our Bachelor's degree, initially both of us were not primarily interested in politics. But by learning more about the challenges of Japan's mature democracy, we became fascinated by policies designed to improve the quality of democracy. Nowadays we both research some shortcomings of liberal democracies: local governments that have problems filling their positions due to the lack of candidates as well as issues of representation because of the lack of female politicians in national as well as local politics. While we chose to concentrate on social science within our Japanese studies program, we did not have any seminars specifically focusing on political systems. Thus, we had to put in considerable effort to read up on democracy studies on our own, trying to find our place as area experts with a focus on political science. Doing interdisciplinary research as a PhD student without formal education in our secondary field came with a proper case of impostor syndrome and we felt lost and not qualified enough to contribute to the study of democracies. Coming from a rather small research field as Japanese studies entering into the larger discipline was rather intimidating. So to say, we have a double outsider status: We are outsiders in the discipline we are engaging with and also outsiders of the country we are studying.

Being a scholar of area studies residing outside the country we study can pose different problems especially to PhD students but senior researchers as well. For one you are always looking for funding (but who is not in academia?) to be able to venture into the field without having to worry about money too much. When starting our doctoral studies, both of us were planning to go to Japan several times[1] during semester breaks to gather data abroad - aware that this would cost us some money but having a position at the university we were sure we could pull it off. When we started our PhD in fall 2019, we were not expecting the global pandemic that started to change all of our lives only months later. Of course, quickly traveling to Japan for research was out of the question only half a year into our PhD. Like so many others we tried to stay motivated and hoped that the pandemic would sooner or later end. We even joked about no matter what happens in the world, a country like Japan can not simply be sealed off, we should be able to somehow venture into the field at some point...or so we thought.[2] It has now been over two years during which it has been either extremely difficult or outright impossible to enter Japan as a non-Japanese and

---

1 Which was, we have to confess, a quite stressful and environmentally unfriendly research design. The issue of research and climate responsibility is now being discussed in greater detail within the German-speaking research community of social science research on Japan as for example the German Association for Social Science Research on Japan does: https://vsjf.net/.

2 History could have warned us, thinking about the long period of heavily regulated international relations in the Edo period (1603-1867) under the Tokugawa Shogunat (1600-1854), where Japan under an isolationist foreign policy closed off almost all harbors to foreign ships only allowing trade with China, Korea, Okinawa, the Ainu, and ships sailing under Dutch flag in a few port towns.

non-resident. This situation has made us and other scholars
of Japanese studies frustrated and scared, but also creative
in terms of how to get data when you cannot get it first hand.
Depending on what kind of data you want to gather,
Japan can be a gold mine or a desert. With some Japanese
language skills quantitative researchers can access tons
of data provided by national and local administrations
but for qualitative research it can be much more difficult.
For example, it takes careful and consistent trust building
and networking to secure an interview with a politician
and getting more than scripted statements that can also
be found in party pamphlets or on official homepages.

Since we were not able to go to Japan, we started to gather
data available online, but the more local the topic becomes
the harder it gets to gather all the information. Social media
has provided exciting new possibilities in the last decade, but
the data is messy and hard to comb through. Doing research
on electoral campaigns, which take place mainly on the
streets in Japan, we were not sure how to start our research
without being able to visit the rallies. Many candidates,
activists, but also bystanders document rallies by taking
videos and uploading them to the internet. Of course this can
not replace being in the field and being able to talk to people
on the ground, but it will at least give you more insight into
the situation on site than newspaper clippings. Nonetheless,
video-clips still come with their own issues of framing.
Fortunately people are also open to new approaches like
online interviews, where you can apply traditional methods
in new settings. You just have to have the courage to try! If
the Covid-19 pandemic taught us anything then to expect the
unexpected. This does not mean to not make plans for working
in the field; contrariwise, solid plans are still the best basis for

change. But we have noticed that the ideal plan will most likely not hold until the end of your research project. It might even only last until your first efforts to venture into the field, at least that is what many of our *senpai*[3] warned us about. But, being flexible not only means to be creative when encountering an obstacle but also to notice an obstacle early when it arises.

So what kind of advice would we give to students interested to pursue an interdisciplinary project between area studies and democracy studies? Well, we would like to share one recommendation and our way of implementing it in our research routine: Stay flexible by building a network with peers. Let us elaborate.

As you are either entertaining the idea of becoming a PhD student or have already commenced your PhD project, you probably already are a flexible, creative person with a knack for problem solving. Make sure to build on this forte. If you are not sure that this is you, do not worry, there is a way to enhance these desirable traits if they do not come naturally, and that is through a network of peers. Building a strong network of peers not only helps you to stay on top of the latest news at your institute or research activities, it also, most importantly, provides emotional support and a safe space to get first feedback on research developments, test new hypotheses and ask the questions you are too afraid to ask anywhere else. Having a small group of peers to confide in is an immense confidence booster without which we probably would not have made it this far. If your neatly outlined research plans goes awry, do not get discouraged, this happens to everyone! Sometimes the best way to get back on track is to actually talk

---

3 The Japanese term for your seniors at school, university and work, and similar institutions, implying (in the best case) a relationship of caring and support.

to people you trust and figure out together how to move on
or to just get some words of encouragement and share your
frustrations. We profited a lot from brainstorming in our
group of four, and are grateful for each of the times someone
eventually had an idea that saved the day![4] Sure the pandemic
situation exacerbates the lone wolf existence of PhD students,
but it does not have to be like that. In our experience every PhD
student is thankful for scholarly exchange, an open ear and a
helpful hand. This peer network can take different forms like
a reading group, a writing circle or just regular exchanges via
video chat or in the university cafeteria. It all depends on your
needs, but make sure to reach out. It will make a difference and
you will be more resilient and adaptable to sudden changes!

---

4 We would like to take the space here to do a shout-out to Anja S. and Jane K., who are
always there for us with academic and emotional support. Thank you so much folks!

(11) Children, Cheese and Commons –
Uniting Theory and Practice

Lukas Peter

lukas.peter@posteo.net

Before I begin with my story as a doctorate, let me shortly explain what has happened since, so that it's easier to understand what happened beforehand. After completing my PhD, I worked for around two years as a postdoc fellow and lecturer at the University of St. Gallen, Switzerland. During this time, I began to question my chances of pursuing a successful academic career and whether or not I would be happy in this situation. And my answers to both of these questions were negative. Already being in my late 30s and being the parent of two children, I didn't want to move away from my family and friends in Zurich, which would have been necessary in the next step of my academic career. And there certainly were numerous other younger, smarter, and more motivated people out there to outcompete me. Finally, I also didn't see myself sitting in front of the computer and reading books for the rest of my life. My regular back pains from desk work and the desire to do something more hands-on made me change my plans – and begin an apprenticeship as a cheese maker. But that's another story. For now, let's return to the question why in the world I wanted to do something so masochistic as write a doctorate thesis in democracy studies in the first place.

As this short biographical note may have already made clear, I never was very sure that going to university, let alone pursuing a doctorate, was really a good idea for me. For I always was very interested in rather concrete activities, like bike riding, carpentry, and farming. But I also realized that getting to the root of things also meant digging into the deeper – and more abstract – questions about life. So, I ended up studying philosophy, pedagogy, and sociology, working parttime in a self-organized day care centre for 6- to 12-year-olds for most of the year and then working in the mountains making cheese during my summer breaks. I ended this life cycle with my master's thesis on freedom and property in the writing of Locke, Kant and Marx.

Then, soon enough, I again asked myself what I wanted to do with my time and energy. My first child was just born and I wanted to do something that enabled me to work from home. And I was somewhat active in a few different political organizations and a community supported agriculture (CSA) project here in Zurich. (For those of you who don't know what CSA means, it is a way to democratically organize our food system, in which producers and consumers negotiate and collectively coordinate their food production and distribution). At the same time, I was reading quite a lot of literature about alternatives to capitalism and came across the concept of the commons. Two reasons for this were that since the finance crisis of 2007/8 there was an increase of interest in "waking Marx from his grave" and in 2009 Elinor Ostrom won the so-called economic nobel prize for her lifelong and in-depth work on the commons. While the theoretical and practical questions that interested me seemed to merge, I also noticed that a specifically philosophical academic discussion on commons seemed to be lacking. As naïve and audacious as I might have been, I then decided that I could fill this gap with a doctorate thesis on the question whether commons may be an answer to the failings of contemporary liberal capitalism.

I then wrote down the idea of my project and applied for a
position as a doctorate student in democracy studies. To my
surprise, I was accepted and thus became a part of NCCR
Democracy, the National Centre of Competence in Research
(NCCR) "Democracy – Challenges to Democracy in the 21st
Century". The awkward thing, however, was that I was one
of the few doctorates who was pursuing an individual project
and therefore didn't really have other people who were
working on the same topic. To make things more difficult,
my main supervisor was an old Marxist, who didn't seem
to get along with my other supervisor, who was a Rawlsian
liberal. And it seemed to me as though both didn't really
like the topic that I was working on. But maybe I am wrong
here, I don't know. To make things even more peculiar,
my second child was then born, and I (luckily) got a job in
a different field, as an assistant in the chair for vocational
education of the pedagogy department at the University of
Zurich. For these reasons, I often felt as though I didn't really
fit in anywhere and when I told people what I was working
on, it sometimes felt as though I was on a different planet.
But maybe that's how most doctorate candidates feel…

Anyhow, the main thing that helped me get through it all was
making friends with a few other doctorates and becoming
a member of a small organization called DemocracyNet
(who also is the publisher of this book). I think it was
both our loneliness and our deep yet diverging interests
in democracy studies that brought us together. Soon
enough, we began not only meeting up for lunch, but also
applying for funding, which then enabled us to organize
numerous (some rather large) events and a few smaller
workshops. Here, we could pursue our individual questions
with others and transform our somewhat theoretical

discussions in the ivory tower into a more public endeavour. In hindsight, it seems as though we were doing nothing other than attempting to democratize our doctorate.

Well, was it worth all the effort? And what can I pass on to other (future) PhD candidates?

Even though I am not in academia anymore, the pain and struggles of writing a doctorate thesis were worth it. Although I didn't end up with any final answers, it did enable me to sort out numerous questions that deeply concerned me. And having these ideas now published as a book is pretty cool! Furthermore, it also taught me to feel okay in the position of not really belonging. And if I can give any advice, it is nothing other than this banality: do what interests you, organize your activities with others and try to enjoy yourself while doing it!

(12) Between Opportunity and Struggle:
The Academic Career in Brazil

Lucas Toshiaki Archangelo Okado
lucas.okado@ufpa.br

I present here a brief report of my academic career. This text is both a confession and an attempt to present some of the context of graduate studies in Brazil from my personal experience. I have to warn readers in advance that this is also a "dated" point of view, in the sense that it is a representation of the current situation, and there are no guarantees that what is portrayed here will be permanent. I hope not.

Brazilian public universities are free and place themselves among the best in the country. However, only a small portion of young people manage to enter in public higher education, because competition is high. Having a lower middle-class background, my family saw education as a form of social mobility. From a very early age, I was encouraged to study and had more opportunities than most Brazilians. In a way, I was privileged.

I entered a social sciences graduation course at a small public state university. In Brazil, social sciences course is a general training in sociology, political science, and anthropology. I think this is a holdover from the French influence in the organization of our higher education here. Before this, I had originally studied to be a teacher of basic education, and had already worked for two years in this role.

To some degree, my academic career then began by chance: I was never a brilliant student, but I had always had a knack for numbers and coding. At the time, a young professor was applying statistics in his research, and, thanks to him, I was able to do my master's and doctorate under his supervision. Today, in addition to be my mentor and co-author in many of my papers, he is also a great friend.

Since the mid-2000s, Brazil has experienced a great expansion in higher education. According to governmental statistics, in 2003 there were 3.94 million vacancies. In 2012 this number practically doubled, reaching 7.04 million in 2012. In the same period, the number of graduate programs in political science jumped from 15 (2003) to 32 (2012). There was a huge shortage of skilled labor in higher education and having a master's or doctorate degree meant a guaranteed job here.

This is perspective that I had started my academic career upon. Higher education had been expanding year by year, there were plenty of jobs and the conditions for doing a graduate degree were very favorable. Here, the bulk of science is done by graduate students. They are the ones who carry out the work in the laboratories and there were plenty of academic scholarships. In addition to being free of tuition, there was the possibility of receiving an income while pursuing a graduate degree.

Thanks to this context, I was able to complete my graduate degree without too many worries. I also received an academic scholarship to spend a part of my doctorate in the United States. In total, all public investment in my education could have bought a small apartment in a medium-sized Brazilian city. Although it had freed me from worrying

about my daily needs, this created an immense personal
pressure. Coming from a developing country, receiving
this volume of resources made me feel that I needed to
find a way to give something back to my country.

At the same time, I had imposter syndrome. I asked
myself on a daily basis if everything I received was fair,
if I deserved all this investment, if I would ever be able to
pay my people back for all these resources that I received,
and if my thesis would be as good as the opportunities I
had. This was accentuated during my stay in the United
States, where I did not really feel worthy to be there.

But from 2012, the scenario changed drastically in Brazil.
The cycle of rising commodity prices ended and public
investment in higher education began to decline. At the
same time, there was a surplus of hyper-qualified labor in
the market, people who had had the opportunity to study at
the best universities in the world. The best academic jobs,
being a professor at a public university, became scarce.

When I finished my PhD in 2018, I came across a scorched
earth scenario in Brazilian science. All the opportunities I
had benefited from before were now practically extinct. And
there was immense competition to get a job. Luckily, I got a
position as a post doc at a university in the Midwestern part
of Brazil, but it was far away from my family and friends.

Between 2018 and 2021 I must have done at least 8 applications
for a permanent position. I have a colleague who did
13! At the end of 2021, when I was already about to give
up my academic career, I was finally called to work at a
university in northern Brazil, in the middle of the Amazon

rainforest. Once again, luck was present in my life. A little bit of my personal competence too. Today I hold a tenure track position at the Universidade Federal do Pará.

The academic career at public universities in Brazil is one of the best in the world: there is stability (tenure), and the earnings are reasonable for the country standards. My generation – those who did their graduated studies between 2005 and 2015 – had plenty of opportunity to qualify themselves. However, the scenario has changed and today, a job in public universities is increasingly scarce. Competition is strong, with cases where there are about 120 PhD graduates applying for just one position!

During my graduate studies, I trained myself in the methodological area. In the past decade, Brazilian political science was in the process of consolidation. The adoption of methodological tools that emerged during the behaviorist revolution only took roots here in the last two decades. Therefore, professionals who had training in statistics tools were in high demand. That is how I managed to stand out among my peers.

In Brazil there is a saying that if advice was something good, it would be sold, and not given. But if I were to give some advice to graduate students, I would not pursue this career today. If this is really a dream, then I would advise you to plan it from a very early stage, seizing all the opportunities that the graduate system offers to students in order to publish in good journals, learn one or two foreign languages and become methodologically qualified. Besides, of course, having perseverance in your goal. The struggle to get a job here is going to be intense in the coming years.

(13) Enjoy the View

Emma Hoes
hoes@ipz.uzh.ch

After having graduated from Utrecht University in Communication and Information Sciences in 2015, I started a Master's in Political Communication at the University of Amsterdam. Looking back, I believe this is where my path towards an academic career began. It was now for the first time that I studied and wrote about topics that truly excited me, and this translated into rising grades, encouraging feedback from professors, all of which together made me decide that was I was not done learning yet. In fact, I felt as if I had just taken the very first steps. I exchanged my home country for Spain, where I pursued a Master's in Political Science at the Autonomous University of Barcelona (UAB). When I was close to finishing the program, I started applying for several kinds of jobs – none of which were a PhD. Various bodies of the European Union and the Dutch government rejected my applications for a number of traineeships.

As I did not know what else to do, I decided to stay in Barcelona and found some job on the side to cover my living expenses. Ultimately, I became a part-time research assistant at the UAB, and while working there, I realized I missed something. I missed writing theses such as the ones for my undergraduate and graduate studies, to dig deep into something and both gain and produce knowledge. Funnily enough, my friends thought there must be something wrong with me (because who on earth misses writing their thesis?), but I knew exactly what this meant. I applied for a

PhD position at the European University Institute (EUI) at the Department of Social and Political Sciences. Under the supervision of Prof. Hanspeter Kriesi, I started my PhD in September 2018, and there has not been a single moment that I have regretted starting this adventure at the EUI.

During first year of my PhD, I wrote a short personal impression for the EUI website and social media channels:

> *"It was a hot, sunny day in August that first day at the EUI. I still remember the amount and diversity of fellow PhD Researchers to be simply overwhelming. [...], I can say that this is one of the aspects of doing my PhD here I enjoy the most. While working on your PhD can typically feel lonely, at the EUI you have the opportunity to present and discuss your work with people from different fields and years, during colloquiums, workshops and seminars. [...]"*

Today – some four years later - I still stand behind what I said then, and I also know that what I wrote does not apply uniquely to the EUI but to many other universities too. What I did not know back then, however, was that the amount and diversity of fellow colleagues were just one aspect of what was overwhelming.

I remember some PhD seminars quite vividly. In class with fellow PhD students, we discussed subjects related to various classical political science theories such as those from Dahl, Schumpeter and Schattschneider. Generally coming from a (political) communication background, I read most of said authors' books for the first time, and some concepts I had never heard of before. Other people in class, however, spoke of these concepts with ease, even reciting what felt to me were complete paragraphs from other classics: "Didn't Achen and Bartels on page 73 of their book published in 2016 mention that [...]." I felt overwhelmed. Walking back home after such classes, I wondered if I was at the right place, and questioned my knowledge thinking I knew too little. I compared myself to others, which in turn made me feel dumb and incapable.

While everybody compares themselves to others for a variety of reasons and it does not need to be harmful or lead to feeling overwhelmed, I wish I had known back then already that – especially during a PhD – this comparing and the insecurities that came with it were not only unnecessary, but also unhelpful as it led me to the wrong conclusions. I recall proposing an idea to my supervisor, outlining my arguments, but finishing with: "But well, I'm not sure, you of course know all of this better." My supervisor replied and said: "No, Emma, I do not, and even if I did, this is not why I took you in as my supervisee."

He went on praising my qualities, some of which had found their home in the back of my head. This was because the predominant thing I had focused on so far, was all that I should have already known, but did not. As best as I could, I stopped comparing myself to others and shifted my focus to what I already knew and – most importantly – wanted to know. It is also only now I realize that not knowing it not only okay, but it can actually be turned into a strength. Do we know X? No. Do I want to find out, do I care, should we care? If the answer is no, I move on. If the answer is yes, this could potentially be the beginning of a new exciting endeavor.

Along with this important step, I also started "celebrating" all successes, and I mean not just the bigger ones (e.g., important deadlines, passing the first year, etc.), but also the smaller ones. Every little step on one's PhD path is important, and even the littlest of steps can feel like miles. I rewarded myself every time I felt I accomplished something: When I finished writing that page that I had been struggling with for a while, when I got accepted into a conference, when I had a productive meeting with my supervisor, or when I got a new idea. Some of these achievements are smaller than others and there are so many more things I could add, but once I was done with something, I crossed it off my to-do list, and took myself out for a nice long walk in the sun, for a coffee at my favorite place, or for a beer with my friends. Doing this made me feel accomplished, no matter whether that was objectively true or not. I reminded myself that it is important how I felt about it all, as – after all – it is you who started and will complete your PhD journey.

I defended my PhD in October 2021, and today I am Postdoctoral Research Fellow at the University of Zurich. The things I have written up in my PhD confessions are ones that I keep practicing every day and at times, still need to remind myself of. An academic career is labor intensive, and if there is one advice I would give those about to embark on their PhD journey, it would be to celebrate all little successes. I believe this is what will keep you going, and helps you keep track of not just the things you want to accomplish, but also what you have already accomplished so far. The PhD mountain ahead may sometimes seem so steep, that all we do is focus on the miles that we still have to climb. In doing so, we at times forget to stand still, look back, and enjoy the view from the considerable heights we have already achieved.

(14) How to have a good PhD Experience: Finding Security and Community

Dominique Wirz
dominique.wirz@unifr.ch

My name is Dominique Wirz, I am a communication scientist and currently a postdoc at the University of Fribourg, where I lead a project on news consumption on Instagram and Tiktok, founded by the Swiss National Science Foundation. The aim of the project is to investigate how entertaining features in news on social media affect exposure to news stories and what individuals learn from the news. Thus, I am not actually a democracy researcher, but my research addresses the question how news media can convey information about current affairs to citizens who have little political interest – which I consider to be quite relevant for a functioning democracy.

I did my PhD at the University of Zurich in the Department of Communication and Media Research. I was employed in a large interdisciplinary research project, the NCCR Democracy. In my research group within that project, we investigated the effects of populist communication on citizens' attitudes. The group consisted of PhDs, a postdoc, and two professors. We were closely collaborating with another team at the same department consisting of one PhD, one postdoc, and one professor. Further, we collaborated with political scientists at the University of Zurich, and communication scientists at the University of Fribourg. My PhD was thus much less solitary than it is for many others – I'll come back to this later.

As a PhD within the NCCR Democracy, I was also enrolled in the Doctoral Program "Democracy Studies". This was (and still is) an interdisciplinary PhD program; there were mainly political scientists in the program, some political philosophers, and some communications scientists. The program had only few requirements; we had a colloquium once a year and needed to visit one thematical and one methodological course at a summer school. These activities only took a small part of my time as a PhD; mainly, I was a trainee in my supervisor's team, which was a group of around ten PhDs and postdocs.

The editors of this book asked me to write about the major challenge I experienced during my PhD. However, looking back with a few years distance, there is no major challenge that comes to my mind. I do not want to say it was always easy, there were difficult moments for sure. But generally speaking, I had a very good time during my PhD, and I think the key factors for this were the security and community I had during this time. What does this mean? With security I mean that I never had a (serious) doubt that I would successfully finish my PhD. The main reason for this is that I was surrounded by people who believed in me. On the one hand, this was my supervisor, and on the other hand my colleagues. I did my PhD at the same University as my Masters, so I knew most of the team before I started. Nevertheless, it was quite competitive to get the PhD position. This paid off; everyone around me was convinced I would do fine. If you do a PhD, make sure to work with people who believe in you. There will for sure be moments of insecurity and doubt, but they will be short if you are in a supportive environment.

The second key factor for me was working in a collaborative project. This meant regular exchange, a lot of feedback, and structure. Of course, it also meant juggling with different expectations and perspectives, finding compromises, and spending time in sometimes inefficient meetings. Even with these downsides, I personally find this much more attractive than working on a solo project. Not only because I profited a lot from working in a well-funded project with renowned scientists; it was this community that kept me motivated all of the time. By the time you start a PhD you should be able to tell of you prefer to work in a team or alone. Choose a setting that allows you to create the working conditions you need. Even if you enjoy the freedom of working on your own, I can only stress the importance of connecting with your peers.

Last but not least, while a PhD is a lot of work and can sometimes be hard and frustrating, it can also be a really good time. The best advice I can give is to enjoy the opportunity to learn from the experts in your field, to have the time to pursue your own ideas, and to meet likeminded people. As you advance in your academic career, these opportunities will get fewer and fewer. Appreciate them while you can!

(15) The Toughest Job of your Life

Jonatas Torresan Marcelino
jonatas.torresan@gmail.com

Beginning a doctoral program could mean you have taken on a considerable challenge. Furthermore, your doctoral studies may be the most challenging job of your life, at least up to that point.

It is not the most demanding job of all. Claiming that would be presumptuous. However, it is no exaggeration to say that a lot of challenges lie ahead, perhaps more than in a conventional job you may have had before. Allow me to list a few reasons:

- The first task is to understand the relevant points already made in academia on the research subject. The classics are a well-known option, but with academic output growing exponentially worldwide, it may not be easy to choose what and how to say next. The risk of forgetting an important finding is ever-present.
- In your thesis, you must find a needle in a haystack in a growing and diverse data field. And data is now rapidly changing – taking on new formats that make analysis more challenging.
- Handling academic output growing exponentially with increasingly complex data, you have to say something new and offer the academic community a plausible explanation for your research problem.
- When companies or governments have a serious problem to solve, they quickly set up a crisis room with many skilled people working together. What

about the doctoral student? You have a blank page
in front of you and a lot of data to analyze.

- But what about congresses, criticism of articles, advisors,
  and colleagues in study groups? All these tools are
  indispensable in the production of a good thesis. At
  the end of the day, however, your thesis will be yours
  alone, and you must make sure that your deadlines
  do not allow you to forget that at any moment.

Of course, all this dramatically increases the pressure
on doctoral students. In addition to any researcher's
obligations in a university, how will you react when things
in the most demanding job in your life go wrong?

The scientific world has recently begun to debate burnout
in universities more seriously. Believe me, many things
can go wrong in your three or four years working on a
thesis. Examples include misguided opinions about the
literature before you read it; methodologies that worked
well for other work but do not function as expected in
yours; the wrong division of time for different chapters
of your thesis; and last but not least, loneliness.

Writing a thesis can be a very lonely job, even if you get on
well with your colleagues at university. If you are in a first-
class university, demanding results of yourself can crush
you as much – or more – than criticism from colleagues.

At some point, exhaustion may set in. If you do triathlons, one
of the most taxing sports events there are, your body may not
respond as you expect during the competition. A doctorate is
a kind of intellectual triathlon. It may demand more of you
than any other academic activity has ever demanded before.

It is a fact that every job requires intellectual effort.
That said, just as different sports have differing demand
levels, so does scholarly work. I believe that academic
careers may be among the most demanding activities
from an intellectual point of view. Your mind may
not be able to handle the pressure at some point.

For a long time, I was one of those people who thought
going to a psychologist or turning to a therapist for
help was an extreme case for people going through
severe problems in their personal life. That's all.

That was until I found myself cornered and exhausted by
my thesis. I was not producing what I had expected and
needed to do, and I decided to seek help from a psychologist.
After a few months of working with a therapist, I recovered
my output, and I managed to finish what I had started.

Do not brush off the professional help of a therapist. Your
intellectual abilities and what you have learned in life are
your raw material. If you do not take care of your emotions
responsibly, you could pay a heavy price - perhaps at a crucial
moment in the thesis. Do not let a time bomb keep ticking.

Finally, writing a thesis is like building a house. Before
you lay the foundations, you need to sit down and think
about whether you have all the necessary resources and
how you will manage them. No one starts a construction
project to leave it halfway through. Take your schedule very
seriously, and understand that it can suffer unexpected
setbacks, just like any job, after all. Setbacks are all right
and inevitable – have a plan B, C, and D. Is writing a thesis
is a difficult job? Yes, like building a house is, too.

However, what drives a researcher are questions, not answers. One way to know if you are making the right decision when beginning a doctorate is to ask yourself: "Do I really want to answer this research question? Will the academic community move forward with the answer to my research question? Will this bring me satisfaction and achievement in my career?"

If this inspires you, get over the difficulties and get on! Just as the drive to see a house finished drives a builder on, the lack of convincing answers to your question will guide your thesis to the end.

Anyone who knows anything about building knows that problems can happen until it is finished. But they are over when the house is ready. Yes, it was difficult, but today this house is finished and is ready for me and anyone who visits.

Your thesis will be a finished house for other researchers and maybe many others from outside academia to visit. This must be one of every good researcher's dreams: to have a home to welcome all kinds of people, not only other researchers living in ivory towers.

I have listed many reasons why doing a doctorate is a tough job. However, as in every profession, we must constantly reflect on the purpose of what we are doing. As scientists, our primary job is to offer explanations and proposals for answers to important questions for society. If that motivates you, a doctorate is the right way to go!

(16) Finding my own Story –
Inside and Outside of Academia

Nina-Kathrin Wienkoop
nina.wienkoop@posteo.de

Born in an overall non-academic family, to pursue a PhD seemed an unavailable goal and therefore, was never something I considered when I was young. Do not get me wrong, I am a great dreamer (to the extent that it often frightened my parents). At the time of my graduation, my biggest dream was to become a politician, which at first glance seems equally far from my point of departure. However, from my point of view, becoming a politician seemed more attainable than becoming a "Dr" of any kind, let alone becoming a professor. Growing up with news programs that dedicate half of the broadcasting time to celebrities, I felt that I did not belong in science. Unlike scientists, politicians appeared more regularly in my daily life – on flyers, on television, next to the entrance of the underground station, on campaign posters (as a democracy scholar I am glad about this experience).

My first encounter with a professor, in return, was at a later stage and rather intimidating. It was initiated by one of my schoolteachers who took us to the University of Hamburg, the city in Northern Germany I grew up in. When I entered the venerable building, it made me feel displaced, but emotionally moved. I sensed that here people worry less about the struggles of everyday life (that I knew well from my single mother), but more about the global and profound challenges of society. I immediately liked it, but also felt that

I did not belong here – a feeling that never truly went away for many years to come. This feeling of not-belonging deepened when we arrived at the large lecture hall. The professor was standing in the auditorium, far away from us – in the proper meaning of the word, but also in its figurative sense. Fortunately, life teaches you to grow beyond your origins, but they will nevertheless always be a part of your very own story, and of your - sometimes misleading - feelings.

For instance, I still remember the moment when I won a scholarship to study abroad during my master degree, and was invited to an introductory meeting for new scholarship holders. At this occasion, I met the director of my university and sat at a round oak table with other "chosen ones". (Many intimidating oak tables will follow where I will feel lost at.) I felt uneasy in my own skin. How should I behave, how should I move, what should I say that portrays my cleverness, and thus justifies my invitation? I repeated in my head, that I shall not talk too loud or too fast, not gesticulate with my hands too much or at all, and, at any circumstance, do not interrupt somebody who speaks. In sum, I told myself not to behave like I was used to behave in my non-bourgeois family. By now, I am able to label this feeling and retrace where it comes from. The famous sociologist Pierre Bourdieu, whose parents were likewise non-academic, imprinted the term of *habitus* to express this knowledge of cultural behavior. This ingrained manner of perceiving the social world surrounding you gives you an early-on socialization that deeply imprints on your behavior. An aspect that is still now often underestimated in understanding why people are excluded, or feel uninvited in the first place. This concept helped me to label and understand what I experienced in countless moments during my studies, and even far more during my PhD.

During my PhD, one day I was sitting in front of a PhD student advisor, desperate because my scholarship was about to end soon after three years, whereas my PhD was not (many will be familiar with this phenomenon). Therefore, I went to her office to figure out if there was any option to apply for an extension or another fellowship. Instead of presenting me with options to help me solve this urgent problem, she asked three questions that irritated me long after our conversation: First, she inquired if my parents were not able to help me out for some months. I was instantly thinking of my mum, who had sometimes worked several jobs in order to provide our basic needs. Again, I felt not at ease and definitely not as if I belonged there. Secondly, she was wondering, if I – who she was reading correctly as a woman – plan to become pregnant any time soon and highlighted the value of pregnancy for the prolongation of my grant. Do not get me wrong, such social securities are essential and should be available for any person who starts a family life while pursuing a PhD. But I *myself* was not telling her about any desire to have children. Third, she asked if I had a boyfriend who is husband-material (whatever this means) because getting married would help me save money. In this very moment, this woman gave me the feeling that the solution is either my family, my gender or my relationship status. Having escaped the tight corset of my childhood, in which many of my girlfriends desired nothing more than having a baby and finding a husband, I felt pushed back there. I had thought that I was now in a different environment, one that is far away from where I started. Several years needed to pass in order for me to understand that this new environment whose habitus felt foreign in many moments, still contained many strings that I tried to leave behind.

The fear of having no money became a constant companion, one that many PhD scholars know very well. This is even more the case if you decide not to take a paid position at the university, or when this option is not accessible to you. I decided to hold on to the scholarship and not to apply for a position. Years later, I perceived my decision as a wise and brave one that allowed me to follow and find my own path, instead of working my ass off for a professor or project. My motive was not only my passion for my freedom, a desire that mismatches my background, but rather my inner deep knowledge that my career will be outside of academia. Although my studies have shown me eventually that I do belong to „the academic circle“, I often felt too enclosed. The narrow structure of „how to write“, „how to cite“ and „how to present“ has always bothered me. And above all, it was too far removed from society, especially from my origins. And this is what brings us back to my starting point.

Coming from a rather hands-on family in which problems are solved practically (or never), I felt too far away from the people – despite studying "the people" and their revolutions in my PhD.[1] This mismatch became the one I struggled the most with. Because a PhD, even in democracy studies, is far from being democratic. The more I became an expert, the further away I felt from the groups I studied. For me knowledge was a way to my own liberation, a treasure to be lifted and passed to others, and, at best, to change the current status quo.

Following this desire, I searched for knowledge transfer and transformation outside of academia. And I found it in many different side jobs during my PhD. I translated my findings

1 Wienkoop, Nina-Kathrin 2020: Social movements as safeguards against democratic backslidings in Africa? A comparison of term amendment struggles in Burkina Faso and Senegal, https://pub-data.leuphana.de/frontdoor/index/index/docId/1079.

into recommendations for political foundations, I built
up networks for a social start-up, I gave advice to German
and European policymakers at a think tank, I helped civil
society organizations to become more diversity sensible,
and I empowered and trained students in their skills. This
manner of following two career pathways at the same time, the
academic and non-academic way, was above all exhausting,
and once again made me feel wrong wherever I was. A feeling
that, to my surprise, many other PhD students share. I think
two aspects are crucial for such feelings: your own biography
- where you come from – and the manner how we define
success. In academia, certain achievements are recognized
while others matter less, or nothing at all. How many peer-
reviewed publications are you able to show off (besides your
PhD, of cause), who you know in the academic circle, and how
much founding for projects you raised. All of these aspects
have nothing to do with real impact on society or politics - in
academic wording, there is no direct impact that statistics
are able to measure. But since I wanted to prove that I do
belong where I was, I followed all those performance criteria
that I knew mattered. I wanted to belong to this cultural
system and perceived it as the only way to go. Therefore, I
did not only follow my very own way outside of academia,
but also tried to prove myself inside academia. It often felt
that the core of my PhD became a side-product that I can
work on after being successful in all other playing fields.

Looking back on this journey, I do have one central but very
strong advice: do not compare your journey to others, always
consider your starting point and, most importantly, enjoy
all the detours. Do not judge the detours as your weaknesses
that you try to hide, but instead value their uniqueness and
the learning opportunity that they offer. Because when I

look back on those years, my detours enriched me in many
ways, personally and professionally. First and foremost,
I met people I would have never met without doing a PhD
(especially not where I came from) – inspiring rappers who
risk their lives for change, widely traveled diplomats at
intimidating oak tables, or enthusiastic young entrepreneurs
who all believed in their visions of a better or at least different
tomorrow. Such detours I often judged as unnecessary
became the clear advantage. By the end of this PhD journey,
I was able to nourish a broad personal network of different
sectors and diverse institutions as well as many skills.

Let me therefore address those PhD students who do not
perceive themselves as academics in the narrow sense: find
your very own story, and in that story, find your skills. Even
if you discover your passion for a non-academic pathway
later on, be aware of the knowledge and skills you acquired
in all those years. We learn so much more during our PhDs
than what can be measured as scholarly success – we learn
how to cooperate in diverse teams, to work interculturally,
to become diversity sensible, to present findings shortly and
(very) intensely, to do an elevator pitch at conferences, to
advise people, to teach, to transfer knowledge, to find funding
for your project and to apply for it, how to manage multiple
projects (or how not to), to write in your mother tongue but
often also in English (if this is not your mother tongue), to
do interviews, to work abroad, to do field work (sometimes)
and so on. This list can be filled with many more skills.

In the end, my very own PhD in democracy studies has
been not only about the people as a power of political
change but about people from diverse backgrounds,
professions, cultures, and places. And, above all, a

reflection of my own habitus and point of departure. This
is maybe a happy end I have never expected, but one that
I keep as my own source of happiness and strong believe
in myself. Now, I feel – at least most of the time – that I can
become whatever I want and create my very own story.

(17) Industry vs. Academia in Democracy Studies. Which Road to Take?

Yani Kartalis

eikartalis@campus.ul.pt

Disclaimer 1: I certainly do not know the definitive answer, nor will I even try to offer one here. It probably depends on each person's needs and goals, is the generic enough answer. However, what I will try to do in the following lines is offer an alternative to this dilemma by talking about my experience.

Disclaimer 2: I am heading to Denmark as I am writing these lines for a postdoc position I accepted. Go figure!..

I did my master's in research in political science which as a program guided most students almost automatically towards a PhD track. As if there was no alternative, and with a slight lack of profound pondering, I myself applied for one and got accepted. The position was within an ERC project, in gorgeous Lisbon and the conditions for my thesis in terms of input were simply amazing. Funding, resources, great PI and colleagues, great institution. So, the output really rested on my efforts. It was an overwhelmingly positive experience that could not easily be matched or surpassed.

Still, ever since I began my journey to my doctoral degree, this question lingered in my head. It was also often the topic of discussion with colleagues at more advanced stages in their careers.

For me it was more of a "am I certain the standard career in academia is what I want?" conundrum. The focus was on whether I liked research in academia as I had experienced it up to that point and not so much in comparison to other viable alternatives outside academia, which are perhaps not many in our field.

I definitely have a broad scientific interest about political science and democracy studies, but I was never, and still am not, particularly interested in answering fundamental questions on my own. Having a formal training that gravitated towards positivist approaches and quantitative methods, I became good at methodology and applying tools. I also quickly became the methods guy within my project and to be honest, I liked it. I am good at listening to other peoples' research ideas and helping them translate them into quantifiable objects and up to this point in my short career, I have worked better when following the lead of other scholars.

But where did that leave me with regards to my "own" research? My PhD research topic certainly seemed very interesting in the beginning. But over time, (like many others might say about theirs), I quickly lost sight of, and interest in it and was spending more time on the project's tasks and deadlines and less on advancing my thesis. This helped me grow immensely in terms of skills, but it took away some of the original research passion towards 'my' research. I was not feeling motivated to work on my thesis.

This was a problem for about two thirds of my journey to getting a PhD. But when it mostly mattered, (i.e. during the last year of my funding) when I HAD TO write and finalize chapters, it all clicked. A series of global disasters, fortunate decisions, and copious amounts of luck led to my last year during my time as a doctoral candidate being the most productive one (for my thesis). I suppose this entire collection might have many stories on the "struggles of getting a PhD during the pandemic" but my story was not like that. I was just lucky to be in a position to take advantage of remote work, distance myself from the project's goals and focus entirely on writing (the part about our job which I do not really love).

This process made me realize that I was really capable and enjoyed working remotely and I wanted this feature in any career no matter the path I would choose. But it also made me re-think how I would make (academic) career choices. What I am trying to say is that my interest for my work/research had severe fluctuations during these years. This might not be a novel observation for PhD candidates and perhaps not even for academics in general. For me it meant that I had to take my needs (be it remote work or interest in the topic) very seriously.

After submitting my final thesis manuscript, I had a variety of postdoc positions available to apply to. But I wasn't sure I wanted to continue. I was also not particularly interested in any of the available options. I knew I needed a break, but my funding ended so I also needed a way to make ends meet.

So what do I do? Go for the available postdocs or maybe get a job outside academia and re-evaluate? I struggled personally and had intense discussions with my mentor and thesis supervisor about this apparent dilemma. She urged me to continue in academia and frowned upon my eventual decision to work for an organization outside of it. We even discussed the "necessity" to leave that position out of my CV when I applied for academic positions. For many, there was only one way forward after defending your PhD and that was the postdoc path to tenure!

In my case, not only was I able to jump back into academia relatively easily (admittedly, my absence was not that prolonged) but I also gathered a lot from this small experience outside this world. The "industry" does generally offer better salary conditions. My earnings and financial position improved significantly from the doctoral student grant years, even within this one year-long stint. I was also much more able to easily distance myself from work and switch off during weekends or other longer periods of time. This was eye-opening and made me realize how a work-life balance is extremely crucial for my personal wellbeing. I even gained skills related to my field.

Academia versus the industry is a simplistic bifurcation of the options available to a PhD graduate. Options are in fact much more fluid, and we are now more than ever in a position to cater to our circumstantial needs by opting for more hybrid paths. Options like working for a think tank or an NGO or even a private company while waiting to find a postdoc that fits your research and career goals are more viable than ever. Especially if you have some universally useful skills. To me, after acknowledging that tenure still seems far away, such options are much more rewarding than jumping to the first postdoc position available at hand.

(18) Choose a Song and Enjoy the Process!

Nino Abzianidze

nina.abzianidze@gmail.com

My name is Nino[1], I am 35 and from Georgia. I recently became an Associated Professor of Political Science at the Georgian Institute of Public Affairs (GIPA) in Tbilisi, Georgia. At the same time, currently, I am a research fellow at the Centre of Social Sciences (CSS), where we dig into the Europeanization discourses in the Georgian media. I like to deal with the issues of political communication in democratizing (frequently ethnically divided) societies. Before settling down in Tbilisi, as a junior academic, I visited a number of universities in Europe: I conducted my postdoctoral research at the departments of political science at Central European University (CEU) in Budapest and the University of Copenhagen, had a research stay at the School of Media and Communications at the University of Leeds (UK), gave lectures at the University of Fribourg and the University of Zurich... But, this whole journey took start with me applying for a PhD in Democracy Studies at NCCR Democracy, University of Zurich.

Why on earth would I choose to do a PhD in Democracy Studies, you ask. In fact, there are two decisions one makes at this point – to do a PhD and to do it in Democracy Studies, or more broadly speaking, in political science. And several factors need to be taken into account for both of these decisions, with the first of the two decisions being more crucial, I guess. After all, the field of interest is more or less defined when one finishes the Master studies. Nevertheless,

---

1 In my home country of Georgia, Nino is a common female name.

doing a PhD in Democracy studies has its particularity – the ambitious feeling of creating new knowledge in and educating students about this big idea of democracy and by that indirectly serving the even bigger idea of making societies better, especially those that are still on their path to democracy.

My decision to apply for a PhD in Zurich was a bit of a peculiar one. I have done my BA and MA studies in Georgia and starting a PhD with this educational baggage at the University of Zurich turned out to be a rather challenging task. To be honest, the opportunity came as an accident. At first, I applied for a two-months long research assistantship at one of the NCCR Democracy projects, which implied collecting data about media landscape in Georgia. At the end of the assistantship I was offered to apply for a PhD position that was opening at that project. Right at the start of my PhD I realized that the next few years were going to be tough – my knowledge of theory was scarce (as in Georgia, we did not have proper access to the English language literature of the field) and my familiarity with methods was almost non-existent. Nevertheless, I started preparing myself emotionally, primarily, for the fact that the toughness would be long and that I should learn to live with this for a while. I frequently say that I almost went through the (second) MA and PhD studies at the same as I really needed to catch up with my colleagues in terms of their knowledge of the field and the research skills. This implied hours, days, months that I spent reading, searching, identifying, figuring out, discussing, then searching and reading again, getting frustrated, realizing that I just read the whole piece of text that was irrelevant, etc. I went as far as getting myself acquainted with the philosophy of social science and having a few week-long visits to Georgia, where I hired a private math teacher to teach me matrix algebra (I needed it as I started learning Social Network Analysis myself).

I find myself extremely lucky that my major challenges during PhD studies were rather of an intellectual and emotional nature. I am aware of the stories when some PhD students face more of the structural challenges related to institutional aspects, major problems in relationship with supervisors, tensions with colleagues and the like. I personally was blessed with the environment in which I did PhD. The institute (IPZ) and the program (NCCR Democracy) with all of its personnel were tremendously supportive and helpful to me. It is true that it was a tremendous challenge to live up to the academic standards of my main supervisor. However, looking at it now, this was exactly what pushed my efforts of making the best I could out of this dissertation. Therefore, the process itself taught me a lot. I also think that it was crucially important to have a second supervisor, who gave a completely different space for discussions, insights and support.

But, of course, we choose to do PhD because beyond challenges, it brings rewards not only of professional nature but also, to a great extent, in terms of personal growth. First of all, it gives a luxury of learning things that cannot be learnt through textbooks. The type of knowledge it gives can only be acquired through experiencing it. Further, PhD studies gave me an opportunity to attend a number of summer schools in research methods, which equipped me with the skills that are valuable also beyond the academic world and can be useful both in private as well as in non-profit sectors. Together with these schools, conferences, research stays and other types of academic activities resulted in a rich network across various countries, which for me has turned into a source of new opportunities more than once. And, hey, that all comes with a lot of travelling! But, for me personally the biggest reward of doing PhD and also the reason why I never regret I did one is the remarkable personal growth that comes with the learning of how to deal with all of the long-term challenges.

I was asked to give one, and only one advice to those who plan to embark on this journey. Well, I have two – one from myself and one form Jay Blumler, one of the fathers of the political communication field, whom I had an opportunity to meet personally during my research stay in Leeds and whose short but powerful advice was a game-changer in terms of how I approached my doctoral dissertation. On a research seminar, after my presentation he asked me if I could tell him in two sentences what my PhD thesis was about. Having seen that I started stumbling with my response, Prof. Blumler suggested to me to exercise in putting the whole idea of my thesis in two sentences. It was exactly as a result of this exercise that I eventually distilled the idea of what the thesis really was about. Therefore, I found this advice to be very useful and these days, I keep giving this advice to everyone who plans to do or is already doing a PhD.

And that one, and only one, advice from myself – in other words, what I would have liked to know when I started my PhD: Enjoy it! It was only by the end of it that I realized that, in fact, I was creating something and that the process of creation, a creative work, if you wish, is a whole different source of pleasure and excitement. I started looking at my manuscript as if it was a sculpture. Some parts of it have already been built by that time but I had to compile others, then to assemble them together in such a way that it made sense as one whole sculpture and then to give it some final touches for the purpose of refining its forms. As I starting enjoying it, this whole process brought me a great feeling of self-fulfilment. The type of self-fulfilment that is hard to reach with any other type of task. I am convinced that this kind of attitude of mine played a major role in why this PhD landed me a Summa cum Laude in the end. By the way, music helped a lot in the process of writing. Try it. You choose the song!

(19) An Interview About not Finishing

Anonymous
interviewed by Christian Ewert
ewert.ch@gmail.com

Introduction

Lea (my co-editor) and I were very interested to give room
to voices who can speak about not finishing a PhD. Because
that happens too. That someone starts but does not finish.
We are sure that every PhD student thinks of quitting at least
once. But some of us decide – and what a difficult decision
that must be! – that not finishing is preferable to continuing.

However, it was difficult to find someone who was
willing to write a confession about not finishing a PhD.
Could it be that still so many emotions are involved?

Having said this, a former PhD candidate agreed to an
interview with me so that I could tell their story. It is only
a second-best solution, as we would have favored a first-
hand telling; but still, given that this particular voice
is important to us, we chose to include it anyway.

The interviewed person read and approved my text
before publication. Text in quotation marks is verbatim,
but translated by myself from German to English.

Lea and I feel very grateful for having the
opportunity to present this interview here.

Background

The interviewed person enrolled as a PhD student in a project they were very interested in. They made the decision to quit after about one year.[1] This was shortly after they had presented their project outline for the first time, which was met with positive feedback. During the interview, the person emphasized that the timing might have been bizarre, given that they quit shortly after having received such good and encouraging comments on their project.

However, the person explained that they were having doubts about their PhD project for a long time before that first presentation.

In the end, they said to have found the courage to quit. Indeed, "finding the courage" was important and emphasized multiple times throughout the interview. One thing that helped them to find this courage was therapy, during which their thoughts about the PhD and quitting were explored.

The person described their supervisor as being calm when they did finally quit. It came certainly as a surprise, given that the supervisor, apparently, did not know about or anticipated the person's doubts regarding their PhD.

Still, the person had to chew on their decision for about two years. One question that kept popping up in their head was: "What would I have needed to stay?" Finally, what has helped them to accept "the new reality" was finding a fulfilling job. Today that person works as a public administrator in an area related to their former PhD topic.

---

1 Which also means that this person never experienced things such as the peer-review process or the revision of the manuscript, which tend to appear at later stages of a PhD project.

The good things
During the first part of the interview, the person mentioned the good things they experienced and what they were able to take away from their time as a PhD student. They talked about the many opportunities to learn. These include of course the more technical or professional aspects, and actually *doing* science. However, other learning opportunities include social skills, or meeting and discussing with other people.

The person also said that they enjoyed the time they had available to dive deeply into a subject of their own choosing. To have freedom to dedicate oneself.

Finally, being able to teach others and to grow as a person were also important.

The things with potential for improvement
Despite these positive experiences, the person also saw "potential for improvement" at university.

Most importantly, the person mentioned "insecurities" while doing a PhD and the "framework" which was not as supportive as it could have been. In addition, the person said that they "usually are not shy," but that they have often refrained from saying anything or expressing their doubts and worries openly.

Another point that contributed to their insecurities is the feedback culture at university. While receiving feedback from peers and supervisors is very common and supposed to improve one's work, the person found this feedback "not always benevolent" or constructive. In general, leadership, supervision, and communication follow

a more "old school approach," which is characterized
by strict hierarchy and "arrogant professors."

Finally, the workload is too high, with both young
and old scholars regularly working until late at night
or during weekends. Indeed, working so much that
almost no time is left for family or private life appears
to be the norm and is even expected at university.

As possible solutions, the person suggested that professors
should train their social competencies more, or that working
groups can create more opportunities for mutual support.

Their decision
What, then, led the person to the difficult decision
to quit their PhD? They mentioned two issues,
the second being the more important one.

First, although they were highly interested in their PhD's topic,
they found their work on this topic almost meaningless and
without impact. This is because most of the work was highly
theoretical (e.g., collecting and reading literature) or simply
unsatisfactory (e.g., spending days upon days on statistical
calculations with little progress). At one point, the person
was asking: "How does this [i.e., the work] benefit society?"

Second, their supervisor and a post-doctoral researcher, who
was also involved in the person's research project, didn't
show "the right kind of support" and leadership. Although
the person was certainly "pushed" to learn more and to be
more productive, they would have wished to have had more
responsive support and leadership, taking into account
their individual needs as a junior researcher. Furthermore,

the person often felt to be in an "environment that was too competitive," and to have received not enough salary for the amount of work they were doing. Finally, the person was often unable "to separate work from non-work" and that they were "thinking about the PhD too often," thus leaving little time or energy left for private life, friends, and family.

As mentioned earlier, the person then found the courage to leave university. Today, they said, they are content with their decision, and that they have found happiness in their new occupation.

(20) My PhD in Darkness

Christian Ewert
ewert.ch@gmail.com

Hello. My name is Chris and I did my PhD in democracy studies from 2013 to 2018. The confession I want to share with you today is about my depression, anxiety, and pain during the second half of my doctoral studies. It was during that time that I met the Darkness.

In 2013 I finished my Master's degree with a reasonable grade and a lot of passion for science. By chance, a PhD position opened up roughly at that time, and it was with some senior researchers I already knew on a topic I was familiar with. I applied without hesitation and was invited to an interview. Which went well, I suppose, given that they invited me to join their team. Even further, and luckily for me, since the project was conducted at two universities, they asked me where I would like to be enrolled. I chose the university in the French part of Switzerland, given that my long-term partner S. had just moved there for her own job and I was looking forward to moving in with her again.

This move was actually a rather big deal for me. I didn't know anybody there besides my partner and the people I worked with, and I left most of my dearest friends in Zurich, where I did my BA and MA. Finally, without being fluent in French, making new friends outside of work proved to be challenging.

Anyway, my project's beginning was very exciting (as every doctoral student will tell you). There was so much to learn.

So many people to meet. So many things to try. For example, the very first conference I attended took place in Jerusalem, Israel, and it was just amazing. All day I had those deeply stimulating discussions with brilliant minds from all over the world, while in the evenings and at night I was exploring this beautiful and enticing city with all its rich history and culture.

I was ready to prove myself. Ready to do the hard work, to research, to write. Me being part of the venerable institution that we call university. I was a scientist.

Things changed, however. Some of these changes were gradual, of course. Stress building up, deadlines approached, more responsibilities to honor, more tasks to complete. Other changes were more discrete. And I started to ask myself questions such as *What am I doing here? Why is this so hard? Why doesn't anything make any sense anymore?* Over time, these questions turned into doubts and self-criticism: *You are not good enough to be here! You will never finish this! Everybody else is so much smarter than you!* In the beginning, these thoughts appeared like shadows in my mind but soon turned into a Darkness that engulfed everything.

No longer did I see myself as a researcher, a writer, or a scientist. Instead, I called myself a loser, a weakling, and a failure. Someone who is unreliable and useless. I felt disgusted by myself.

The last six months before defending my thesis were the worst time in my life. Literally. I had to rework my script based on my jury's feedback, and I felt alone, inadequate, so miserable, and afraid. Constantly afraid. There was only pain, and I drank way too much just to make it go away.[1] Not sure who exactly but someone said that having depression feels like drowning, except that everybody else seems to have no difficulties breathing at all.

To be honest, I really don't recall many details of these six months. They appear as just a blurry mess with no day being any different than any other. I remember, however, my partner S. and how she was holding me when I was crying, how she reminded me to eat, how she was worried about my health. In hindsight, I understand that she was struggling with my situation at least as much as I was. How helpless she must have felt.

I think of the Darkness as an illness and hence don't want to attribute blame to anyone. However, from discussions with other (young) academics I know that I am not the only one at university who is or was fighting with anxiety, loneliness, stress, self-doubt, and other mental health issues.

It was impossible to open up to my supervisors, jury members, or mentors. It was impossible because I didn't think of them as being available or responsive regarding my emotional needs. I cannot remember that doubts, feeling, worries, or the like were ever acknowledged in our discussions.

Even today, I remember vividly the few episodes when I did try to reach out and speak with authenticity and truth. When I wanted to share my vulnerabilities or ask for help. It took all my courage to approach the people I worked with to truly connect, but there was no empathy or comfort to be found in their responses. For example, one academic said to me: "You're lucky and very privileged that I even

____

1 I sometimes said that a certain Captain Morgan had become my second supervisor.

spend my time with a junior researcher like you." To me
this was soul crushing. Consequently, I retreated more and
more. I couldn't manage the presence of others anymore.

In the end, my thesis didn't receive any honors or
praise. It did not make any impact. It is not a testament
to my intellect or commitment. It is best forgotten.

After defending the PhD I was hoping to feel better and
started a post-doc. Yet, having never sought out therapy,
the Darkness stayed with me. For example, I began a
promising research project with a young and passionate
scientist called D. Working with her was just so exciting,
and we had so many ideas and visions. But whenever it was
my turn to actually write for our paper, all those crippling
thoughts of mine about worthiness (or the lack thereof)
came back. And to this day it still haunts me that I was
unable to push this project and the paper (which remains
unpublished) as much as I wanted to. Since then, I have long
given up on having an academic career as a researcher.[2]

It took me almost three years to really get better. During this
time, I enjoyed the random non-academic discussions and
interactions with friends, for example with my fellow scientist
and coach J. And slowly I started to notice that there was an
alternative to the pain, that my life didn't have to be that way,
and that – maybe, just maybe – it was possible to live outside
the Darkness. And once I had noticed that, I kind of decided
for myself that I wanted to have that other life. That I had
enough of misery and despair, and that I wanted peace and

____

2 Although I still do have the privilege of teaching at the Department of Political
Science, University of Zurich. In fact, being able to teach and work with students is
one of the best things that has ever happened to me. I would love to do this for many
years to come.

joy instead. And then one day, I decided to just step out of the Darkness. Of course this is a metaphor and the transformation took much much longer and required much much more effort than a simple step. But to be honest, today it *feels* like I have finally stepped out of the Darkness. Today I feel alive again.

And today I can share my feelings, my worries, my anxieties. And I can talk about my time in Darkness.

There is not much advice I can offer. Of course depression and anxiety are illnesses, and professional help is available and effective. Please do not neglect your own mental health, and look out to other people as well. Many universities offer psychological consultations for students and staff. Many countries have emergency hotlines and crisis counseling that are available 24/7.

But if I may, I want to end this text saying thank you. I was lucky enough to have met the right persons at the right time, like the three people mentioned in this text. And you and others have reached out to me when I was swallowed by the Darkness. You have grabbed my hand and just never let it go. I was not always able to say how much you and your support mean to me. But I had suicidal thoughts once or twice in the Darkness. And I don't know whether I would still be here today if it wasn't for you.

(21) Always get a Sparring Partner

Caroline Dalmus
caroline.dalmus@fhgr.ch

Why on earth would anyone choose to do a PhD in democracy studies? To be honest, as so often in my life, the decision to do the PhD was rather spontaneous than thought through thoroughly. I am not the kind of person with a five- or even ten-year plan knowing exactly the goals she wants to achieve. Instead, I look for opportunities that come up in life and decide rather intuitively if a certain (career) path is attractive to me. After I had finished my master's degree in Communication Research and Media Studies at the University of Fribourg, Switzerland, I was kind of lucky that three new professors were hired, all looking for potential PhD candidates. Since I had always been interested in courses focusing on political communication during my studies, I applied for the PhD position offered in this area. The job interview went very well and a couple of weeks later the position as research assistant at the University of Fribourg was mine.

I was really exited but also a bit scared because I had no clue how to start the search for my PhD topic. Thus, it was a relief when my supervisor told me that I should apply for a PhD program in Democracy Studies. Of course, finding a suitable topic was still a challenge, but at least the program offered me a structure that helped me to organize myself and set milestones. What I enjoyed most during the program was the possibility to regularly present my PhD project and its progress to other PhDs and researchers. This was especially important for me, since I was my supervisor's sole PhD candidate and thus never really had a sparring partner with whom I could discuss ideas and problems. To be honest, quite often this was very frustrating for me, because I saw how much colleagues at bigger chairs profited from the exchange with their colleagues. What made the PhD program in Democracy Studies so valuable to me were the multiple perspectives due to the heterogeneity of research areas integrated in the program. While computational linguists always challenged my thinking about methodological aspects of my research, the political philosophers came up with questions and ideas I would have never thought about in my wildest dreams.

The feedback I received was essential for my progress and overall, the critical discourse made me feel good about myself and my PhD project. However, I also had to experience how criticism that is not constructive can have quite the opposite effect. Unluckily, I had to make this experience during my first presentation not even three months after I had started with my PhD. Due to the short amount of time I had to prepare the first draft of my PhD outline, the concept was vague, the research questions broad and the theoretical foundation superficial. I had hoped for some inspiration in which direction I could go, but instead the feedback from the researcher discussing my proposal devastated me. After a couple of minutes, I wanted to run out of the room, and after a couple of minutes more I wanted to quit my PhD. I do not know what his intentions were, if he simply had a bad day or if he is a person that needs to decry others in order to feel good about himself. But what I do know is how severe the damage of nonconstructive criticism can be. Not only does it make you feel bad, but it also steels valuable time. Time, in which you should be working on your PhD but instead are caught up in self-doubt.

In a perfect world, such people wouldn't exist. However, reality is different. Even though a majority of researchers is complaisant and constructive, there will always be idiots (at the moment I cannot think of a more appropriate word) at each conference, in each research project, in each committee deciding on funding. And even though you are prepared for this, their comments will hurt, make you angry and sometimes even question yourself. Especially, if you are not part of a big chair or research team with many doctoral students and post-docs with whom you can discuss the feedback and who will mentally support you and build you up. Thus, if you are part of a small team and more or less "alone" with your supervisor, I would highly recommend you to actively search for sparring partners right at the beginning of your PhD. I missed this chance and always tried to solve my PhD-related problems alone. Having sparring partners would have helped me to pay less attention to harsh voices and more strongly focus on the many critical voices that were constructive and offered solutions. Maybe even my attitude towards a post-doc position would have been more positive. After finishing my PhD, I was so happy to leave the traditional scientific career path and a post-doc was the last thing I wanted to do.

Even though a position as a post-doc was no option for me, I did not want to quit working in the scientific field completely. Today, I work at a university of applied sciences as project leader and scientific researcher and taking this job was the best decision for me personally. My daily routine is very multifaceted since I undertake applied research projects with many different commercial partners besides my regular teaching activities. Additionally, I have time reserved for scientific research projects and I can enjoy the benefits of working in bigger teams that strongly engage in discourse and productive exchange of perspectives and knowledge. Thus, I am even more convinced that one should make sure to be surrounded by sparring partners. In fact, the benefit is twofold: on the hand, sparring partners make thinking about problems and developing ideas so much easier, because they widen your perspective, let you see alternative pathways and can help handling critical aspects of your research. On the other hand, they can support you when dealing with nonconstructive feedback, because they surely have experienced it themselves and thus are able to put such feedback into perspective, build you up, if necessary, and sometimes even make you laugh about it.

(22) It Takes a Village

Susana Rogeiro Nina
susana.rogeiro.nina@ulusofona.pt

When I was invited to write my confession, my first thought was "Oh my God, the PhD again!" and the second was "In which way can I specially contribute?"

Then I looked at the clutter in my living room, with my three-year-old son's toys scattered around, and the frightening amount of papers that remain untidy since the last shutdown, and realized "I'm a woman, I'm a mother and I carried out my PhD during a pandemic, with a baby to take care of, and that alone is already special!".

Obviously, my PhD is not limited to this sentence, but it is, without a doubt, one of its hallmarks.

I often say that doing a PhD resembles a love relationship. The first year is the period of falling in love, of passion, in which we look at our topic as the most important and most surprising thing in life. We want to shout out to the world how relevant, fantastic and unique our research question is. We repeat until exhaustion that we love what we do and that we know exactly which research design we are willing to follow. At this stage we are sure that we have made the right decision by starting a PhD, and that no obstacle will be too difficult to overcome.

However, as everything in life, early (or not so early, as in my case) we realize that doing a PhD is not just studying a topic we love. And little by little, the butterflies in my belly

and the enthusiasm that once characterized my days as a
PhD student, gave way to routine and some disenchantment.
The enthusiasm we used to feel when we talked about our
research is gradually replaced by a series of uncertainties,
anxieties and insecurities that make us ask ourselves
what we are doing there, what we were thinking of when
we chose this topic, or why we chose this for our life.

 I remember one day, after hours of unsuccessfully trying
to build an argument, I wished I had been much more
modest in my ambitions and condemned myself for not
having chosen a much simpler professional career.

Don't think I regret having done a PhD. Actually, I loved
doing my PhD, I love the subject I researched, I love
doing research and teaching, and I genuinely know that
it was the best decision I have ever made. However, I
would like to ask you to do the following exercise:

Imagine an 18-month-old baby born during the second year
of the thesis. Then imagine being persistently haunted by a
history of failures of my institution concerning students who
became parents during a PhD and who never finished it. Add
to this a pandemic that forced us to stay confined at home
and adapt to a new reality, where the routines that used to
provide us with security and predictability had disappeared
Let's face it: this could be the perfect recipe for chaos!

The anguish of knowing that the day only has 24 hours and
that in those 24 hours I had to be a mother, a wife, a researcher
and write my thesis was enormous. Time didn't stretch and
everything seemed to be unbalanced: if I was writing the
thesis, I couldn't take care of my son; it I was taking care of my

son, I couldn't write the thesis. It was the moment when I hated my PhD the most and when I really regretted having defied the odds and having a child during a PhD. However, it was also the moment when I realized that I would have to write my thesis no matter what, for myself and for the love I dedicate to my son.

Looking back, sometimes I still wonder how I managed to get my PhD in the allotted time, how I managed to write a thesis in the middle of a pandemic, defend it, have a career, and keep my sanity. It almost looks like an oxymoron. Nevertheless, I think the answer is much simpler than it seems.

To do a PhD we need a village. A village of people who motivate us, who believe in us, who celebrate our successes and suffer our failures, who, in the end, provide us with the resilience that keeps disappearing.

Talk to these people, look for these people! Whether they are your supervisor, your co-supervisor, PhD colleagues, friends, family, the gentleman who sells you bread every morning… it doesn't matter. The important thing is that these people make us fall in love again with our PhD, with our research, and make us laugh at ourselves for ever having wished to work on something else.

And don't be doubtful: that passion comes back, even when we already think it will never happen. Returning to the metaphor of the love relationship, it is the moment we feel the rekindling of the initial flame. Eventually not with the same ecstasy or enthusiasm as at first. But that's good! We start to look at our PhD with a greater dose of realism, serenity, and a sense of the way to follow, with our feet on the ground.

One day, a very special person told me that doing a PhD
is a marathon and not a sprint. You must manage the
effort along the way. It was the greatest advice I have ever
been given. I recognize that it is not easy to understand
it, not even to put into practice. But it's true, doing a PhD
is either a long marathon or a long walk. Sometimes you
have to stop. A month, two months, as long as it takes,
to regain energy and come back. The process is hard,
I cannot deny, and my experience proves it, but in the
end, it is so rewarding that it makes it all worth it.

One last confidence, as a piece of advice: When you have been
told that you are not capable or that you have the odds against
you, think of what you really want and just do it. I assure you
that you will make it and will prove everyone and yourself that
the margin of error can be much bigger than others assume.

(23) Relive them Millions of Times: My Years as a PhD Researcher

Jessica DiCocco
jessicadicocco@gmail.com

I don't know exactly how it came to my mind to devote myself to democracy studies. I only know that there was a moment in my life when I realised that I would like to do research in this field. Until then, the idea of doing a PhD had been remote, if not absent, in my mind. Indeed, I had always shown a particular passion for the more practical issues related to democracy, the mechanisms of voting, active participation in social movements, and voters' attitudes. But if ten years ago someone told me that I would end up doing a PhD, I would have barely believed it. Instead, it happened. Happened that one day I realised that I wanted to research populism, electoral behaviour, and party leaders, even if I still didn't know how. After winning a position as a PhD student at the Socio-Economic and Statistical Studies EuroPhD at Sapienza University, I entered the academic realm. I was attracted by this doctoral course's interdisciplinary nature and empirical orientation. I vividly remember the excitement I felt when I read the ranking list and discovered that I had won a place on a scholarship, which was a necessary condition for me. My first day as a PhD student is also etched in my memory. I remember walking briskly down the long avenue of the university campus straight onto the department of Economics. My adventure began from that 'vintage' building in Via del Castro Laurenziano in Rome.

When I think of my PhD years, I am filled with a whirlwind
of emotions and discordant thoughts. One always thinks
of how cool making research is, but the reality is that not
everything that glitters is gold. The PhD years are beautiful
and stimulating but also very tiring and demanding. It is not
trivial to figure out how to manage your time. You have to
understand how to put your ideas into practice, learn how
to do research, and occasionally redraw its boundaries to
make it feasible. There's a nice cartoon representing the PhD
project as a beautiful castle, while the application of the PhD
project is a sandcastle.[1] There is no point denying it; there is
some truth to this metaphor. You think your project is cool,
innovative, and cutting edge. Despite this, you still have to deal
with the timing and what you can actually achieve with your
resources. I had to reschedule my plans several times due to
lack of suitable data, unexpected results or external factors.

Just to mention one example, when the pandemic broke
out in 2020, I was about to start the last part of my research
project with my thesis due in October that year. This part
involved collecting data through a lab experiment. As
you can imagine, that period in history was not exactly
the best for conducting experiments with several people
in closed rooms. When I realised that I had to change my
plans, a workaholic urge came over me. I started working
at an unbearable pace, trying out different analyses,
restlessly changing my questions. In the end, I found an
alternative idea that met my needs and ambitions reasonably
well, but not without stress and enormous fatigue. The
delivery of the thesis indeed was a liberating moment,

1 https://www.facebook.com/MemingPhD/
photos/a.2165566000354385/3186900924887549/

especially as I had already won a post-doctoral position and did not suffer the 'what will I do now' anxiety.

Loneliness is another familiar feeling in PhD life. It happened to many fellow researchers; it occurred to me too. The relationship with the supervisors can sometimes be Machiavellian, and you can feel lonely, almost abandoned in your research. You are always on the borderline between being a rib of a professor and being a mind that works autonomously, exchanging ideas with the supervisor. There is no right way to live your position as a PhD student; it depends on you, how you are, and your needs. Gender bias, speaking as a woman, remains another thorny issue. There has been an improvement, but other work has to be done for gender equality in the academic world. I noticed a first cap to overcome; if you succeed, you're done, and you're in the Olympus of women who have succeeded.

Furthermore, if you like interdisciplinarity like me, you will probably know that interdisciplinary interests in research can also be a challenge. As an interdisciplinary scholar, you have to consider a staggering amount of information and habits that belong to different disciplines, trying to channel them all into your research. This can be hard, especially when there is no single accepted definition of concepts, like in democracy studies. Doing research in democracy studies while spanning interdisciplinary fields and controversial topics is as stimulating as it is frightening. It can happen that you don't feel like neither fish nor fowl. In my case, I was not totally a political scientist nor totally an economist. I'll let you imagine how difficult it was to define myself when a third label, that of computational social scientist, was perhaps added to these two labels. Of course, every field has its specific interdisciplinary challenges. For example, suppose you investigate populism using computational tools. In that case, you still have to bear in mind how essential definition issues and categorisations can be, even if you are interested in testing empirical hypotheses rather than theoretical aspects.

However, despite the terror, the pressure, the procrastination, the doubts, the unanswered questions, the last-minute changes, the PhD years gave me a satisfaction that can hardly be reported. The further I went on my journey, the more I realised that my mind opened a little more each day. I grew up as a person and as a scholar, finally becoming able to question my own ideas and beliefs. I gradually learnt how to put together the pieces of the socio-democratic and economic puzzle we live in. I also experienced new ways to talk about my job with lifelong friends or family members, avoiding the temptation to analyse them by inferring political positions or behavioural attitudes. Perhaps because the topics in question are so shared, everyone creates their own beliefs and thoughts about politics, democracy and populism. Hence, there's a substantial risk that even dinner with friends turns into an opportunity for research.

I could go on with other anecdotes and other considerations, but I think the focal point is what I would suggest to someone who intends to undertake a PhD in democracy studies. I have thought for a long time about this aspect and finally got to a conclusion. My suggestion is to look with curiosity at the world around you while developing the ability to detach yourself when you risk going into an 'infodemic'. It may sound silly, but your brain performs much better after a good night's sleep or a relaxing outing, while giving you less satisfaction after hours and hours of lockdown on books

and papers. Take care of yourself with the same dedication
you employ writing your thesis, and you will experience
a win-to-win game. And learn to love your research, your
time as a researcher, and your very own bizarre curious
perspective on the world. As I always say, the doctoral years
were the worst years of my life, but also the ones that I
would like to relive millions of times. Take care of them.

(24) Fishing a PhD in Times of Crisis: A Generational Experience

**Camila Farias da Silva, Eduardo Georjão Fernandes &
Matheus Mazzilli Pereira**
camilafsb@yahoo.com.br
eduardo.g.fernandes@gmail.com
matheus.mazzilli@gmail.com

Science in Brazil is heavily dependent on governmental investments. Research funding is concentrated in public federal universities (with a notable exception for the public universities of the state of São Paulo) that are free from tuition charges in all levels. Scholarships for graduate and undergraduate students as well as post-doctoral fellowships are also mostly dependent on governmental policies for higher education.

When we started our formation as researchers – as undergraduate students between 2007 and 2008 and graduate students between 2012 and 2014 – this scenario worked in our favor. At that moment, Brazilian universities were perhaps in their "golden age". The left-wing federal administrations of the Workers' Party (*Partido dos Trabalhadores* – PT) conceived the development of higher education not only as an educational or science and technology policy, but also as a tool against the dramatic social inequalities of the Brazilian society. Making the best of a period of economic stability, investments in research grants and fellowships peaked. The federal government founded new higher education institutions, opening teaching positions for junior researchers. Public policies aimed at broadening the access to the universities, such as scholarships for low-income students in private institutions and affirmative actions in public universities, promised to finally democratize higher education in Brazil, historically mostly restricted to white students from upper and middle classes. The future was promising.

However, this future did not last long. In the final years of the Workers' Party administrations, between 2015 and 2016, both an economic crisis and austerity policies diminished the levels of federal investments in higher education. After the deposition of President Dilma Rousseff (PT) (described by many Brazilian social scientists as a soft coup) and the rise of a right-wing coalition in the federal government, budget cuts in this and other policy areas increased. With the election of the far-right Jair Bolsonaro in 2018, not only resources became increasingly scarce, but also science started to be targeted by systematic offensives of the ruling coalition. Not only the humanities and social sciences were attacked, criticized by its imagined "Marxist indoctrination" and promotion of "gender ideology," but also to the natural sciences, targeted by anti-vaccine campaigns during the Covid-19 pandemic.

The promised future vanished before our eyes. We were formed as social scientists maybe during the best moment to have done so. Nevertheless, we have finished our academic formation, between 2018 and 2021, during one of the most intense crises in the recent history of higher education in Brazil. This of course generates a variety of frustrations, uncertainties and dilemmas that affect our wellbeing (specially our mental health) given the limited opportunities and the increased competitiveness of the academic job market, fueled by an unprecedented number of new doctors, products of the "golden age" of Brazilian science a few years before.

The first of these frustrations refers to the "promise" of financial stability. We as many other colleagues have imagined during our formation that to acquire a master's degree or a PhD would mean to later access well-paid job positions. And even though the level of education still certainly affects income, accessing those jobs and reaching financial stability is no longer a certainty. When we face this new reality, a question inevitably arises in our minds: Was it worth the effort?

A second dilemma refers to a kind of "territorial instability" in our careers. Given the current limited opportunities in the academic field, it became increasingly hard to develop a career in your home city or state. In the national territory (and the reader must remember Brazil is a country of continental dimensions), there is a frequent transit between regions, given that many contracts are temporary, and few states concentrate most of the job opportunities. Additionally, many junior researchers look for positions abroad, creating a "brain drain" (*fuga de cérebros*) in Brazilian science. If this scenario provides us with the possibility to expand our networks beyond our local restrictions, it also results in insecurity and instability regarding our living situation, hampering long-term plans. After all, where will I be living in the next few years? How will those plans align with the needs and objectives of the ones with whom I'm living, such as children and partners? How will my life-course be affected by the distance with relatives and friends?

Financial and territorial instability tend to have implications for our relationships. The unexpected low financial returns of investments in education in the short term might frustrate the expectations of our families, generating incomprehension between us and our relatives. The possible transit between cities, states, and even countries makes our affective relations more unstable. The short period spent in a location might hamper the development of more durable relations if we so desire. Another question appears in our minds: am I disappointing someone?

Given those problems, it is inevitable to question our "bet" in the academic career in the first place. In many areas of knowledge – and this is the case of the social sciences – the academic career seems to be the most "natural" one. Alternative careers are rarely addressed during our formation as social scientists. However, given the few open positions in the field, it appears that all the tools we have been equipped with during our studies become useless. To sustain the "bet" on the academic career, it is necessary to show high productivity, research and teaching experience, and time for preparing for the tests that regulate the access to positions in public universities. Yet the doubt remains: Even if I fulfill all these expectations of the academic job market, will my efforts be rewarded? Have I been looking for the right job?

To face those frustrations, uncertainties, and dilemmas, we have tried to find "paths" that could turn the life of junior researchers in Brazil economically and emotionally sustainable. The first of those "paths" is the construction and consolidation of networks of support and share. In the social sciences, it is common for our work and research routines to be lonely enterprises, which might create feelings of social isolation and competitiveness towards our colleagues. Opposing these tendencies, we have sought to strengthen our ties with colleagues through cooperation-based initiatives, such as research groups, collective projects, and texts (such as this one). The collectivization of work helps us to appease

insecurities and to show us that we are not alone. Networks
of support also involve the socialization with friends, family,
among others. An important way of dealing with the numerous
demands of the academic life is to avoid them to produce an
excessive feeling of guilt and self-charge, as in the feeling
that we should always be working. Moments of leisure and
affective relations (in their many forms) are fundamental
for preserving our mental health and our self-care.

Besides, we have been trying to diversify our professional
"bets" in the strictly academic field and beyond it. We have
realized that the "expected path" of the academic life (finishing
a PhD and soon after becoming professor at a renowned
university) is not the only possible one. The research skills
we develop might be applied to other work fields and there
are many possible professional experiences out there. If we
take our trajectories together, since we have finished our
PhDs, academically, we have worked as temporary professors
in federal universities, as professors at smaller private
institutions, and as post-doctoral fellows in research centers.
In not strictly academic fields, some of us have worked as
teachers in secondary schools and others have created an
NGO dedicated to social research, which provides research
services for public and private organizations. In the end, even
in times of crises, we have realized that there are many spaces
that value and demand the knowledge and skills of social
scientists. Our challenge is to occupy them having in mind an
orientation towards cooperation and mutual and self-care.

Besides that, we believe it is urgent to seriously debate our
policies and attitudes towards graduate students and post-doc
fellows in Brazil. Since they are both not considered formal
workers, they have virtually none of the rights workers are

entitled to in Brazil, such as vacation, transportation vouchers, bonus salary at the end of the year, formal contribution to the social security system, among others. There are currently no policies regulating how or when graduate and post-doc scholarships are readjusted. We are writing this chapter in 2022 and by now the last time the value of the federal grants increased was in 2013. Estimates from the National Association of Graduate Students (ANPG) suggest that those fellowships have lost approximately 66% of their purchase value due to inflation during this period. The absence of those rights and regulations especially affects low-income students, much more numerous in the Brazilian universities nowadays since the consolidation of affirmative actions. Is it enough to grant them access to the higher education institutions and later low financial support for them to follow their academic trajectories and compete with middle- and upper-class students?

Graduate students and pots-doc fellows must be seen as workers and their activities must be recognized as the essential contributions they are to the academic system in Brazil. Scholarships must not be conceived as "governmental favors" generously conceded for them. The demands and the political mobilization of graduate students and post-doc fellows should not be considered as mere "complaints" of ungrateful students but recognized as part of a struggle for the rights of young academic workers and part of a more general struggle to transform the higher institutions in Brazil towards greater diversity, inclusion, and social justice.

Part C

*

Accompanying a PhD

This last section deals with "the other side" of the PhD experience, that is, with those who support PhD candidates on their journey. Supervisors, of course, but also coaches, trainers, families and partners. We wanted to know what these people have learned from working with or supporting PhD candidates. What is it like supporting a PhD, in a personal or a professional capacity? What are the stories of those "in the background," who are crucial to the success of a PhD journey? How did they come to interact with PhD candidates? What are the enjoyable and the difficult parts of assisting PhDs? Some authors are academics and established professors, others have never worked in research themselves. We asked them all if they can give any advice, both to PhD candidates, and to those who work with them or live with them. What would they have liked to know when they started supporting PhD students? What is the best way to care and encourage at the same time?

(25) In Good Company

Eva Anduiza
eva.anduiza@uab.cat

Throughout my academic life I often found myself reading intensely for research and teaching purposes, but mentoring and PhD supervision have been somewhat more on the practical side of things. A bit like parenthood, I was thrown into it without much training or awareness. It is an attractive challenge to sit down and order my thoughts about this important part of my work as a professor.

It comes in all shades of colors because every person is different, but overall and after witnessing the development of 22 PhD dissertations and the growth of many young academics, I must confess there are few activities in my academic life that have been as gratifying as PhD supervision, and, more generally, mentoring.

It is not only how much you learn from young scholars, which of course you do, and it's fantastic. It is also that you change your view of what this job is about. Being a full professor is not any longer only about you getting things done. It is increasingly about facilitating that other people get them done too in the best possible way, and about trying to enact the conditions that would allow for better teaching and research overall in our academic institutions. From a more narcissistic perspective mentoring and supervising are a different way to feed the voracious ego all academics have. At some point, success and leadership are measured not (only) by your own personal achievements, but by your perceived ability to facilitate the growth of future academic leaders and successful researchers around you. Of course, the merit is entirely theirs, but you feel it a bit as if it were yours too.

There are a few things I have learned in these years of mentoring PhD students which are not as evident from the usual guidelines on "how to supervise". First, a supervisor must find the right balance between letting the student follow her path (a path that is necessarily different than the professors' and sometimes not of her liking) and identifying the quicksand traps to avoid. It is hard to distinguish the very innovative idea that can lead to a first-class paper from the twist in the plot that keeps the student working for months on a crazy idea that leads to nothing. And we never know beforehand, because initially both may look very much alike. I remember my own advisor, Stefano Bartolini, telling me "don't go this way, it will be a mess." He said it only once, although I am sure he disagreed with many of my choices. I think he was right. Since then, I try to remember that, as a supervisor, you are not there to put too many sticks into wheels, nor to lead on a short leash, but that you should be a sort of safety net and ensure completion.

Second, the PhD supervision should be an entry point for the student not only to your own expertise as supervisor, but to the expertise of many other people: people that are important in the student's field of research, the broader research team and peers in the institution where the thesis is written, potential mentors for research stays in other universities, committee members, professors that may be recruiting postdocs or assistant professors, etc. An important part of the mentoring job is helping the student build and strengthen her own academic network. The supervision and mentoring process is not a bilateral relation, but rather the construction of a web where the supervisor is a (temporary) central node.

Postdocs and junior professors are important actors here. Postdocs are "closer" to PhD students than senior professors are in many ways. In fact, to be perfectly honest I think my PhD students learn most from the postdoctoral researchers and junior professors around them. Postdocs and junior professors are "the upper crust" in terms of academic excellence (every generation is better than the previous one, as a professor once made me note) but also in terms of commitment and enthusiasm. Students considering professors for supervision should bear in mind that young is good, and this is not only an intuition[1].

Third, mentoring does not end with the Ph.D. Postdocs should continue to seek mentoring, and complementarity between graduate and postgraduate mentors is important[2]. I consider mentoring post-doctoral researchers as the prize you get after supervising graduate students, a bit like enjoying grandchildren after parenting, to continue with the initial metaphor. It is enjoyable because collaboration in research and teaching is done in a more peer-like relation, but also because as a professor you are given the opportunity to work with them in the development of other skills that will eventually help them to lead teams and mentor their own students.

---

1 Heinisch, D. P., & Buenstorf, G. (2018). The next generation (plus one): An analysis of doctoral students' academic fecundity based on a novel approach to advisor identification. Scientometrics, 117(1), 351–380. https://doi.org/10.1007/s11192-018-2840-5.

2 Liénard, J. F., Achakulvisut, T., Acuna, D. E., & David, S. V. (2018). Intellectual synthesis in mentorship determines success in academic careers. Nature Communications, 9(1), 4840. https://doi.org/10.1038/s41467-018-07034-y

Postdoc positions are also a particularly delicate moment in the academic career, as many female researchers become mothers at this stage. This poses an important and not sufficiently acknowledged toll on their productivity and ability to keep their networks growing. Many consider dropping out because of the contradictory pressures they suffer between academic and family commitments, and all are exhausted. Mentoring becomes crucial in this situation in as far as it can contribute actively to avoid a loss of talent that our universities and societies suffer but cannot afford.

(26) PhD Research in Democracy Studies –
A Confession by a PhD Supervisor

André Bächtiger

andre.baechtiger@sowi.uni-stuttgart.de

My approach to PhD supervision is perhaps a bit old-fashioned: less emphasis on institutionalized structures (in form of PhD programs and schools), more emphasis on personal exchange, (international) networks as well as self-motivation and creativity (even though I think that institutional structures can critically enhance this approach!). The "personal-exchange" approach was also the one adopted by my PhD supervisor, the late Jürg Steiner. We had intensive discussions on the PhD from the beginning to the end. I remember wonderful (and hour-long) gatherings at his home where Jürg wanted to know where I exactly was with my PhD, carefully listened to my report and always "accepted" my crazy ideas (sometimes grudgingly, I know) – and just waited until I found out myself that these ideas were dead-ends. In addition, he sent me to major conferences at a very early stage of my PhD career – such as a conference on federalism at Princeton University to present a common paper. I have tried to "copy-paste" his approach to PhD supervision (even though I strongly doubt whether I am an equally good "listener" as Jürg). On the one hand, I try to continuously give constructive and extensive feedback to the ongoing work of the PhD students, especially with an eye on finding a persuasive storyline that is in accordance with the empirical data but also stimulating from a theoretical point of view. On the other hand, I motivate them to go to as many summer/winter schools and conferences as possible as well as establish a large network of international contacts. Going to these schools and conferences is not only crucial for packing up ideas into written form (with a deadline) and getting critical feedback, it also plays a vital role for familiarizing PhD students with the rituals of the community as well as getting to know people who frequently become life-long friends. Finally, I also encourage them to spend time at another university to hear and familiarize themselves with ideas radically different from the ones they get at my research unit. In sum, I want them to become young scholars with an own identifiable agenda as well as making them "feel home" in the academic business.

At the same time, the academic business in political science has changed massively. When I wrote my PhD, the expectation was that one starts publishing articles when the PhD is close to be finished. By contrast, the current academic business requires that PhD students publish early on. I try to encourage - and especially support - my PhD students from the beginning to produce potentially publishable articles as well as devise a smart and feasible publication strategy. This entails, for instance, publishing promising ideas and/or first data in appropriate outlets and then try to "land" results of finished theses in the top journals.

The most critical moment in my work as a supervisor was when one of my PhD students found out that another scholar had pursued a similar research idea and already had a paper under review (which was also published soon after). We sat together, immediately realized that the project of the PhD student was still very different in theoretical orientation and empirical design, and decided to do two things: (1) contact the scholar immediately and give information about the project of the PhD student; (2) get a publication out of the PhD student´s project as quickly as possible. This was a success at both fronts: contacting the other scholar not only allowed to more clearly delineate the differences between the two research endeavors but also provided the PhD student with further excellent feedback; and the PhD scholar not only managed to get first results out quickly, the finished research also landed in a top outlet.

If I could give one piece of advice to those who work with or support PhD students, then it would be this: believe in their stunning self-motivation and immense creativity but always listen to their concerns carefully, accept that they do things differently, and try to anticipate as well as give them every support they need. In a way, this emulates the surprising success of the internal workings of deliberative democratic innovations (one of my research areas): citizens are not only more motivated to deliberate about political affairs but are also much more capable to do so than many skeptics have proclaimed. But at the same time, citizens have diverse speech cultures, want to be treated with respect, and their motivation and energy to participate and deliberate requires adequate institutional support (good information and good structuration of the discussion). Having supervised PhD students for more than a decade, I think that PhD students in the field of democracy research want and need exactly the same.

(27) What does it mean for a Father to Support his Son Doing a Doctoral Thesis?

Ernst Strebel
strebel.koelliken@bluewin.ch

Retrospect of the father on the doctoral period of the son
I don't think that we as parents provided any direct "support" for our son M.'s doctoral studies. Certainly not financially, he was independent in this respect.

I occasionally asked how the work was going, trying to get an idea of the topics and goals of the research. These inquiries – and this was important for me – were completely free of worries, of anxiety. My impression was that M. worked in an environment in which he felt comfortable, in which he was met with goodwill, in which he was respected, where he could get the inputs and advice he needed. I felt that he belonged to a "community" that extended far beyond Zurich, and which was characterized by mutual respect. If M. said something about his doctoral advisor, he mentioned the supervisor's first name; he was on a first-name basis with him. The supervisor's role as a mentor and, finally, as an evaluator, did not exclude cooperation as partners in certain areas. If I remember correctly, there were some projects on which they worked together, to which M., under less time pressure than the Prof, contributed even more. M. also participated in congresses during the doctoral period and was able to publish articles in journals. He had been encouraged to do so, I think, by his PhD supervisor. As a biological father, I was impressed how my son's life circles expanded, how city names such as Mannheim, Vancouver, Chicago, Amsterdam, and others became stations on a professional path.

I heard little about work problems, about doubts, about periods of slackness, which certainly also existed, and perhaps I asked (too?) little, because the basic conviction that "he can do it independently of us/of me" was strong. What we did talk about occasionally was our different ways of approaching things that were pending, or of starting the day: The son's tendency to postpone sometimes and to be efficient only under a certain pressure (but without missing deadlines) was contrasted by the father's compulsion to immediately do everything that was pending; the tendency to stay comfortably under the covers for a while was contrasted by the urge to wake up and immediately take a hot and cold shower.

More involvement, more curiosity than the scientific work process aroused in me the life circumstances, of which the professional work was only a part: the life in the shared apartment, the peers who were close to him, the place of work (e.g., the shared office with an Italian colleague), the everyday life in Mannheim, dealing with the separation from the life partner during several weeks, getting to know other young scientists at congresses, the informal happenings at such gatherings. And, of course, to notice that yet another doctoral student joined "our" doctoral student and soon also sat down at the family table: Our life world expanded and was greatly enriched. So that ultimately the question would have to be reversed: What does it mean, for an old man, to be supported by his son and by his son's partner? The answer would be the facial expression of one who can hardly find adequate words for the meaning of this vital support.

**Retrospect of the father on his own time
as a doctoral student (1978 – 1983)**

I took up my dissertation topic, after studying up to the
licentiate in Bern, with a Zurich professor whom I knew only
by hearsay, about half a year after I had started with a part-
time job at two cantonal schools and a Jungian psychoanalysis.
As with all of them, the beginning of teaching involved a
great deal of preparatory work. In addition, between 1978
and 1981 I also took the necessary courses, internships and
exams for the "Höhere Lehramt" (secondary school teacher
diploma). The consequence of all this was that I worked on
the dissertation almost only during the school vacations,
never really got into the subject (evaluation of German
translations of Italian poetry of the 20th century), went to
the professor about once a year and reported on the little I
had done. One of the topics of the psychoanalysis was – very
simplified – to free myself from superego obedience, to take
my own feelings more seriously. Especially in the last phase
of my dissertation, I kept thinking that I needed the academic
title to satisfy my superego, to increase my self-worth. With
psychoanalytic irritation, I reflected on this constellation
and fretted that I was not secure and courageous enough to
let the doctoral work be (though there was already genuine
interest in the subject matter). – After four years, I realized
that I would have to take half a year of unpaid leave if I ever
wanted to finish the dissertation, a financial sacrifice (at that
time a good 30'000 Swiss francs) that I could afford because
my wife taught full time at an elementary school. That half
year was the best part of my dissertation time: I worked for
two and a half months in Florence, met once with a professor
in Urbino and with a Viennese professor at a congress in San
Remo, had to go to Munich for a few days for research: A little
bit of the outside world came into my life as a librarian.

My relationship with my doctoral advisor was one of distant reverence and suppressed rebelliousness. Even in San Remo, I almost didn't dare to ask the professor from Vienna to send me his paper, and I was then totally delighted how nice he was, how accommodating. During the five years of work on my dissertation I had hardly anyone to talk to about my scientific activities, but after the publication of the dissertation (in the most inexpensive form possible at that time) there were a few pleasant reactions (I sent copies to a few professors and cultural journalists who had published in my subject area). This brought me offers of collaboration with scientific journals, especially from the Viennese professor of Romance languages and literature; he also arranged for me to participate in a congress in Düsseldorf. After a period of illness, which today would probably be called burnout, I almost completely gave up scientific work, and wanted to use the time I had left, besides my professional and household days, for my fiction writing, and was only occasionally active as a consultant for translators.

Conclusion

When I compare my son's years as a doctoral student with my own, I see a positive development in the academic working world. The inhibiting hierarchical thinking (on the part of the professor and the student) has, so it seems to me, given way to an interaction between the scientific researchers that is characterized by more partnership. Moreover, while writing a dissertation in social science and the humanities used to be a mostly solitary (and expensive) affair, it now takes place in a communicative context and is often associated with a remuneration roughly equivalent to a basic income. These are, in my view, important advances.

(28) From Worries to Solutions –
What I Learned from Coaching Academics

Christian Ewert
ewert.ch@gmail.com

Hey there. My name is Chris and after I had finished my PhD, and to complement my research, teaching, and writing, I have started to work as a coach. My clients come from all walks of life and I also work with academics such as master students, doctoral candidates, post-docs, and professors.

In this chapter I want to share some of the lessons I have learned as a coach. And although each PhD "journey" is unique, and everybody makes their own unique experiences and has to find their own way, there are some issues or worries that come up in my work with doctoral candidates regularly.

Before I talk about these issues and worries, you should know that people come to me when they need or want support and help. They talk to me about situations when they struggle or that they find difficult to cope with. My job, then, is to help them find solutions, to help them remember how strong they really are, to re-discover their own inner strengths. Coaching is supposed to be an encouraging and safe process of transformation, which does begin with worries but ends with solutions, strategies, and empowerment.

Consequently, as a coach I mostly see the "ugly" side of university. I see people burning out. People crippled by fear or self-doubt. Dreams and hopes shattered and

discarded. There is no doubt that work at university can
be rewarding and fulfilling. But it can also be ugly.

Supervisor

The relationship between doctoral candidate and supervisor
is probably the number one topic of my academic clients.
And this is maybe no surprise. After all, candidates,
especially at the beginning of their doctorate, tend to
look up to their supervisors and have high expectations.
For one, universities are very hierarchical institutions
and professors have a high degree of authority (too much
actually, if you ask me). Supervisors (and to a lesser extent
the other members of the doctoral jury) can literally make
or break a candidate. And although I know (ex-)candidates
who speak highly of their (former) supervisors, I know even
more who are or were deeply afraid or resentful of them.

Apart from authority, candidates look up to supervisors
because we have learned to do so. Aren't professors
supposed to be experts with brilliant minds, representing
the pinnacle of human intellect, and with answers to every
question? If anything, obviously, professors are humans
like everybody else, neither omniscient nor infallible.
But sometimes it takes a while to understand this.

Hence, supervisor and candidate often have very
different expectations about their relationship,
their needs and desires. I often wish supervisors and
candidates would listen more to each other, and be more
open and engaging. It would benefit them both.

Loneliness
It is true that PhD candidates meet many interesting
people such as scientists, peers, interview partners,
study participants, and so on. But still, reading and
writing, which are two of the main activities in
science, are usually done alone. Working *alone* on
a challenging topic for many years is difficult.

Papers and the review process
Publishing papers in scientific journals or chapters in books
usually involves a peer-review process, which tends to be
anonymous. In short, a text is submitted to the outlet, and the
editor(s) will have a (brief) look at it. If they are interested, they
will send the text to reviewers who are usually experts in the
area that the text is addressing. These experts read the text as
well and give recommendations, based on which the editor
will reject the text, ask for a revision, or approves publication.

This whole process is anonymous, and neither does
the author know who the reviewers are nor do the
reviewers know who the author is. In theory, anonymity
is beneficial because the text is evaluated based on its
own merits. Relationships between author and reviewers
cannot play a role because nobody knows anybody.

One of the issues with the peer-review, however, is that
people often become mean and discouraging when they
are anonymous. In addition, peer-review is a duty that
many scientists find distracting and unpleasant, and hence
they don't invest as much time or care in their reviews.

It often takes time, a lot of effort, and "soul" to write a
paper or chapter. Imagine submitting a text that you've

worked on for a long time. And then you wait for a couple of
months. And then you get the editor's response, including
the reviewers' comments. Sometimes these comments
are helpful and encouraging. And sometimes they are just
crushing and devastating, as they seem to devalue your work.

Teaching and presenting
Teaching (in front of students) and presenting (in front
of peers) are two similar activities that trouble many
academics. They don't like to be in the spotlight, and
feel exposed. "What if my students ask a question I
cannot answer?" "What if I say something stupid and
embarrass myself?" These are typical self-doubts that
arise when people think about teaching or presenting.

Personally, I always feel proud of (especially young) people
when they show up and let themselves be seen. Who stand
in front of an audience and let their voices be heard.

In a way, teaching and presenting, and any other form of
communication really, is like riding a bicycle. It's a skill
you have to learn. It's something you have to practice,
something which becomes easier with practice. And over
time, it's even something that can become enjoyable.

Self-doubt and anxieties
The university is a high-pressure environment. As said earlier,
it's very hierarchical. In addition, many contracts, if not
most, are only temporary, while tenured positions are limited
in number and availability. Consequently, competition is
extreme, and an old academic saying goes "publish or perish"
– meaning that you must constantly produce results and
publications in order to have a chance at an academic career.

In my experience, some folks are able to mitigate this
pressure by creating supportive and trusting communities.
Elsewhere, this pressure hits like a truck. And if it
does, self-doubts and anxieties often follow suit.

Productivity

Many scholars struggle with procrastination. Meaning
they're not doing the things they should be doing right now.
Instead of writing their paper, they watch Netflix. Instead
of reading literature, they play video games. Instead of
preparing the next class, they go shopping for things they
don't need. In the end they're stressed out because the
deadline is approaching and they haven't even started yet.

Procrastination is high among academics, which is
not surprising. If you work at university, you often
have to self-organize your own schedule and tasks.
Further, work at the university is highly abstract and
has a long return-on-investment (it can take years
before a paper is published). Finally, humans tend to
slack off, especially when supervision is lacking.

Strategies and solutions

Of course there are solutions and strategies that can help with
the issues mentioned above. What you should know is that
we all need to find our own solutions and strategies. Each one
of us is unique, and there is no one-size-fits-all. What works
for your friend might be useless to you, and vice versa. Given
this, I can only outline general ideas at this point. So keep an
open mind. And try things out if they resonate with you.

(1) Do sports. Seriously. I know that this book is about
academic endeavors, but if positive psychology has taught

us anything, it is that physical activity is the number one contributor to well-being. So join a team and play soccer, rugby, volleyball, whatever. Or if you want to do something on your own, go jogging, cycling, swimming, whatever.

(2) Join a doctoral program. They help by giving more structure to your PhD journey and connecting you with peers.

(3) Get a supervising contract. Offered or even demanded now by more and more universities, a supervising contract lists expectations, rights, and duties of supervisor and candidate.

(4) Make friends. As a PhD candidate, you're not a lone wolf. Friends can be supportive. And fun.

(5) Do things on the side. There is a life outside of university. Don't miss it.

(6) Take care of yourself and others. We all need to wind down, we all need self-care. And be supportive of others. They too might be struggling.

(7) Get help. Don't be afraid or ashamed to ask for help. It is not a sign of weakness. And remember, if something doesn't feel right, it probably isn't. So if you are in need ask a friend, or find a coach or therapist. We're here for you.

As said earlier, work at university can have an ugly side. But never forget that it can be rewarding and fulfilling too. I hope you will find your way.

(29) On Discovering new Worlds, Making wise Decisions, and Listening to your Cousin

Verity Elston

verity@portfolio-formation.ch

I was 29 when I started my PhD. I'd taken the circuitous route, dropping out of my first attempt at university after high school, doing better the second time around. And in the meantime, working in all kinds of places, in all kinds of roles. From international finance in the City of London to a remote goldmine in the Western Australian desert. From running campaigns in a start-up in Dublin to projects in a research institute in Chicago. By the time I got to the end of my PhD in my mid-thirties, I'd seen a pretty wide range of places and knew fairly well just what fit, and what didn't. (Although I was still perfectly capable of making some bad choices. But at least I knew how to get out of them.)

Doing a doctorate had brought me many things. A perspective and a clarity on issues that intrigued me. The resilience to bring a solo project to a successful conclusion. Fluency in a third language. Yet there was another thing I knew by the end of my PhD: I was in a crowded field and nearly ten years older than the many talented minds in it. If I wanted to take the academic career path, it was going to be a hard scrabble. But to be honest, it was fairly clear that I wasn't all that interested in the uncertainty and the low pay. The moving around and the desperate hopes for the next grant, the next post. And to be more honest still, I wasn't all that enamored of full-time research anymore.

I was certain though that there'd be one thing I could do, given my experience and what I'd looked at in my research. And since I was now living just down the road from Geneva, I was sure that all I had to do was send them my CV and those international organisations and non-profits would open their arms to me. So I did. And they didn't.

"If this is what you really want to do, you're going to have to network," said my cousin, who was at that point in the third of the international organisations he would work for. Hundreds, if not thousands, of people apply from all around the world, he pointed out, and many of them highly qualified. Get out there and talk to people, learn more about the process, get small contracts and hear about posts before they're advertised: this was what was going to make the difference.

But I was an introvert with principles and a nicely laid out CV. I really didn't want to hear my cousin's wise words. So I kept sending in my applications, and kept getting rejected. Or more to the point, not hearing anything at all. It got very, very disheartening. I began to wonder what on earth I was doing with my life. And maybe I should have taken up that "we'll probably find you something" offer of a postdoc in New Zealand? Networking, you see, was not the thing I did. Surely my CV should stand for itself? My motivations, my knowledge and my expertise would be all that mattered. I couldn't stand the thought of engaging in some kind commercial exchange, of you-scratch-my-back-I'll-scratch-yours. Even though so much of what I'd done professionally had been through connections and conversations and keeping an eye out for what people needed and where.

Today, in my work supporting doctoral and postdoctoral researchers about their next career moves, I hear lots of people repeat the same words back to me. Surely the process should be transparent enough and open enough and merit-based enough that an application will get you in where you want to be? The idea of networking, the very word, seems somehow distasteful and degrading. All we need to do is get the right formula of content on the CV, find that wow factor for the motivation letter, and all will be well.

Like many moments of inspiration though, neither the right formula nor the wow factor will come solely from our heads. Creativity and ideas need nourishment from the outside. As do good decisions. How many of us would buy a new laptop or a bike or anything that entailed significant cost without finding at least cursory data to inform our choice? Yet, despite the trained researchers we are, so many of us will take a job ad as the only source of information with which to put together our application. We dare not ask questions. We avoid seeking out the very information that will help us understand why we're motivated for *this* post, how our knowledge and skills could support *this* employer.

Yet having a conversation can reveal and instruct in so many ways, for different types and shapes of organization. Sometimes the person you speak to will indeed be the key to unlocking the job you were looking for. Most of the time though, the route is a lot more complex. Talking to someone may mean just that: having a conversation, learning about where they work and what they do. What the issues are that their organisation faces. The kinds of skills and knowledge it needs. As you learn the idioms and vocabulary other universes use to talk about what matters to them, you begin to work out how to translate from your known language to theirs. How your expertise could support what they do. It's the kind of knowledge that helps craft the CV towards what your employer is looking for, feeds the inspiration to express your motivation in a cover letter that engages rather than bores, and helps you better interact with your potential employer in an interview. It can help you to be "in the right place, at the right time" to learn about opportunities when they happen. And, perhaps most importantly, it gives you the information to make better decisions about what you should be doing next: whether this role is right, whether the organization fits.

But of course, if this pragmatic reason were all that mattered, it probably wouldn't feel so daunting. If we were motivated only by such concrete results, wouldn't we all heed my cousin's advice?

My suggestion is to think of the ways in which we can interact with others that feel more normal to us. To forget the image we might have of networking as standing in a room full of strangers, holding tight to a cup of coffee and desperately trying to think of something mind-blowingly fabulous to say (or even to say anything at all). To put aside for a while the phrase "I need a job", and instead, to reach out to people who do interesting things or in intriguing places, to ask them more about their world. We can find opportunities to interact on common ground with people we do not know already. To take a class or join an association or play a sport that puts us in touch with new worlds – and mediates the exchange by having a topic in common. To allow the conversation to build with the trust.

What if we used the very fact of our introversion, our natural curiosity, our tendency to observe and listen, rather than

speak? If we thought of networking as a conversation? As a way
to ask questions and to learn more about another world? All
the things we do naturally as researchers, without thinking
twice. After all, if you turned this moment around; if *you* were
the person someone was stepping out of *their* comfort zone
to reach out and start a conversation with you, how would
you feel? Embarrassed? Or happy that someone wanted to
learn more about your world, and what interests you?

(30) The PhD Thesis in the Room –
A Partner's Perspective

Bartek Kowalik
bk.kowalik@gmail.com

Those who have lived with someone working on their PhD will surely understand what I'm about to tell here. A PhD is undoubtedly a long process, full of self-doubt, despair, tears, sweat, nightmares, and an entire spectrum of feelings from peaks of happiness to feeling so down that nothing cheers you up. But while this is happening, we don't question the reasons and we can't think of solutions, because we're so deep inside of this rollercoaster and don't want to get out until the ride is over.

Daniel and I met in Berlin where he did his PhD in Political Science and International Relations, working on domestic factors impacting foreign-policy decisions of Brazil towards China. How do I know that? Because I heard about it every single day. The PhD topic seems to consume you, absorb so much of your free time, especially towards the end of the thesis, that it becomes an integral part of your life and of those who surround you. At the end, you are of course the biggest expert in the subject! But on the way there are endless papers, conferences, workshops, presentations and hundreds of other forms of free-of-charge work before you get to the glorious day of the defence. And guess what – each of those conferences, workshops and presentations have to be trained, some in front of the audience, other in the next room. I must admit that by the end of Daniel's PhD, when someone asked me what the topic was, I was able to speak for one hour about foreign policy of Brazil towards China with specific examples and even some International Relations' theories which are, just to be clear, very far from my own area of expertise.

I remember many situations where in the middle of a conversation, Daniel would just stand up and go take some notes of "this perfect sentence for the thesis" or "this great idea" he needed to include. This shows that the brain never stops thinking and processing information, a.k.a. 24/7 service. I also remember him waking up at night and thinking about this one paragraph that may be not yet ideal. Let's not forget about the stress of all the presentations in front of the demanding crowd that wants to eat you alive. And self-doubt if what you wrote is enough, or that someone will publish a paper or thesis on a similar topic making the thesis outdated. And then there is the most stressful of them all: the relationship with the supervisor who can make it or break it for your entire future career in academia. Another thing that we tend to easily forget but that can cause a massive headache is the actual printing of the thesis. Hundreds of pages ready to be submitted and yet here and there a comma or dot missing, the graphs could be better aligned, then reprint, further correction, repeat, repeat, and repeat, until you run out of time and the final product just has to be perfect. And the defence! A bunch of experts looking for holes in your work of the last few years, asking creative, tough questions which you must address on the spot.

But it was not all challenging. There were happy moments along the way: international conferences which allowed cool travels, a research stay in China, which was culturally mind-blowing, all the successes harvested along the way (which were not mine of course, but also a little bit mine), the international folks we got to meet throughout the years and with many of whom we're still close friends, and every little celebration which led to the final goal – maybe comparable with building pyramids. I think the best part for the supporting party is actually the pride. Watching the whole thing come together, all the conferences where you don't understand much, but it sounds so smart, seeing the appreciation for the efforts and then the result makes the partners so proud and makes them feel like they participated in the journey. Which is probably one of the reasons why they will never want to do a PhD on their own.

From the perspective of this experience, I would recommend future PhD candidates to prepare themselves mentally for a long, exhausting journey where their self-esteem and persistence will constantly be tested, to surround themselves with a support network to share celebrations and frustrations, and to find a structured routine. By structured routine, I mean a working space outside of the living space, defined working hours and planned venting activities, and a clear plan that can be pursued step-by-step.

(31) Step Forward: Insights from Training PhDs

Maura Hannon
maura@karnarn.com

I felt like I had circled back when I started in professional
PhD training six years ago. I adored immensely being
at university and living in the world of ideas but walked
out of a PhD program in political economics in my
twenties because I had no shoes. It's true! The heel on
my last pair was badly worn on one side and though
the ideas should have sustained me, I was simply done
with living on air sandwiches and in poor footwear.

Feeling like a failure and a traitor, I volunteered one full
day a week in the Western Australian State Parliament.
Six weeks later I was offered a permanent position writing
speeches for parliament, campaigning at the state and
national levels, and preparing media door stops. Several
stimulating jobs and an MBA later I followed the love
of my life to Switzerland and used the same strategy to
land a job with an international innovation company.

Fast forward through years of raising a young family and
building an independent career in a foreign country I
was asked to present a workshop to PhDs on structuring
writing in English. Thrilled by the prospect of being back in
university halls, I continue to make no secret of how much
I love working with doctoral and postdoctoral candidates,
throwing an outrageous amount of energy into it. Today
I give several workshops a year on English writing skills
productivity, creating LinkedIn profiles and building digital

skill competences. It has been my good fortune to accompany many smart and capable PhDs for a short moment and I derive enormous satisfaction from the thought that I might have played a tiny role in pushing knowledge further.

My career and personal paths have been similar to many of the candidates I've met: job instability; searching for my niche in or out of academia; moving hemisphere; learning a new language; identifying transferable skills to pivot a new career direction. My career has been a journey that looks straight only from the rear view mirror. Although I abandoned my great masterpiece for some creature comforts, I would offer four humble insights from my own experiences laced with collective conversations from the PhDs I have met.

Insight 1: Love your research, but not too much!
A PhD is a marathon commitment to stay focussed on the tiny details of an idea. It can be exciting, frustrating and all encompassing but, because so much of your time, energy and self go into it, your identity can be swallowed by the process. In some cases this can lead to mental health issues. For others, it can create, let's call them, big picture problems. For example many people lead with their potential qualification as their introduction to the outside: "I am a PhD candidate." This one label seems to block a cascade of other questions such as: What do I want? Where am I going next? How am I going to get there?

Insight 2: You are now a professional. Own it.
In or out of academia, a PhD is a job and hopefully it will be one of many to come. The work of a PhD is a clear step into the professional world. You are leading the project of your research with all the budgeting, planning, research and dissemination skills needed. Yes, we are all lifelong learners,

but I actively encourage PhDs who call themselves "student" to find a better label like candidate, researcher or a descriptor with which they are comfortable. The problem with the "s" word is it can carry stereotypes that undersell what you are doing because students are not always agents of their destiny. You also wont need to tell anyone you are a professional because we are all going to just take that bit for granted.

Insight 3: They're gonna ask, so have something ready
PhDs answer in three main ways that icky, picky, sticky question: what is your PhD about? Some will tell you their research is too complex to explain, which always leaves me feeling I'm being kindly told I am not smart enough to understand. Then there are those who start to explain and spiral headlong into an exhaustive and increasing level of complex details (Please! Make it stop!).

The third group have a few simple sentences ready they can adjust to tell grandma, the conference organizer or that chance meeting with your research rockstar. The point is people will ask whether you like it or not, so have something - even if your are still not rock solid certain about it - ready. The bonus here is you can eventually use this text to lead on your CV, online profiles, and, it might even help clarify what's going on in your own head.

Insight 4: It's for life, not just your PhD
I worked in motorsports for a few years and racers will all tell you the same thing: you move toward whatever your eyes are looking at, so set your gaze where you want to be next. Where are your eyes during your PhD? You don't need to know exactly where you want to be, but if your eyes are at your feet I guarantee you won't be in

motion. Here's a good example. I had a postdoc ask once
if six weeks before the two-year contract ended was too
early to start networking for the next position? Umm...

As much as I love doing what I do, I still don't know what I want
to be when I grow up! But I put hope into doing the groundwork
of developing a strong set of skills, creating networks and
opportunities, and trying to vaguely visualize the sort of
thing I would like to be doing in five years time. More than
once I have ended up somewhere else doing something totally
different - but in my experience, planning and visualizing
creates movement. It's the motion that is important because
it will take you somewhere. Stagnation simply smells.

Advice

The one piece of advice I would offer PhDs comes at the
risk of self promotion. Not once in my career have I been
given the opportunity to attend the breadth and wealth of
trainings that most Doctoral programs offer through the
campus. When I tell colleagues about the skill trainings
available, most are wide-eyed with envy! Yes, you have a
lot to do. Yes, it is difficult to get the time off you need to go.
Nevertheless, attend as many of those skill-training workshops
as you can, to ensure your shoes will never wear out.

Conclusions

Lea Heyne
lea.heyne@ics.ulisboa.pt

The first thing that we need to say here is a very big thank you – to all the amazing people that have made this project possible by writing a chapter. All the authors have not just agreed to give us the time it takes to write that chapter, but also to share their experiences, ideas, and insights, often on a deeply personal level. Chris and I were incredibly impressed by the willingness of our colleagues and friends to contribute their stories, and by the creativity and dedication that went into each single "confession." Thank you, to all the authors, for your trust and support.

And the second thing that Chris and I realized when we started reading the chapters, and hearing back from authors, is that the process of writing a personal story like this – be it about the reasons to study democracy, the experience of doing a PhD, or of working with PhD candidates – can feel like a relief, and maybe even be therapeutic. Many authors have told us that reflecting on their experiences and their paths, sometimes difficult and even traumatic, sometimes very positive and empowering, has helped them to make sense of their own story. And this is certainly true for us, the editors, as well – this book has felt more personal than anything we have ever published before, and it feels like a great way to acknowledge and learn from our personal experiences.

There are some interesting observations we've made during the process of finding authors for this book project. First, many senior researchers that we have asked to contribute here declined or didn't even answer. This is of course partly due to the fact that as a professor one tends to be incredibly busy and receive far too many emails and proposals – we completely understand that. But we also had the impression that the topic and approach of this book was not something that seemed particularly attractive to senior academics. There are, of course, exceptions, and we are even more grateful to those professors who despite a high workload took the time to share their story with us. At the same time, most young(er) researchers that we contacted where immediately and incredibly passionate about contributing here, and very much liked the idea of this project. Maybe the closer one still is to the PhD experience, the more one feels the need to talk about it?

At the same time, we are also very happy to have the great input of young and innovative democracy researchers in the first part of the book. People who see democracy not just as a field of study, but who try to challenge and redefine what democracy means and how and where it should be applied. After all, how can we research democracy professionally if we don't also aim to democratize our mindsets, our understanding of who gets to have a say in talking about democracy, and our workplace – academia – as well?

A second observation we've made is that those former or current PhD candidates, who we have asked to join but who have declined to write a chapter, did so for two very specific reasons: either because, as they said, their PhD experience was so "boring" or uneventful that they have nothing to write about, or because it was so traumatic that they simply can't. As a result, we probably have collected stories that exclude both the best (assuming that an uneventful PhD is a good PhD) as well as the worst experiences. Nevertheless, we feel that there is a large variety of stories – people who have struggled with internal issues or with external barriers, and people who have found or created good conditions for themselves to thrive during and after the PhD. And despite the very different backgrounds and conditions, some things seem to affect all those who shared "the PhD journey:" the initial excitement, the search for community and belonging, the importance of a supportive network both on a personal and on a professional level, the self-doubts, the personal growth when overcoming obstacles.

Third, it has probably been the hardest to find contributions for the section on working with PhD candidates. We tried to find people who have the reputation of being "good" supervisors, and we asked around a lot, asked colleagues at many different institutions. And yet, we only got very, very few names. Most people, even if not unhappy with their own supervision experiences, hesitated to "recommend" their supervisor. Does this mean that most supervisors are doing a bad job? Certainly not, but it did make us wonder what is going on here. Maybe we've asked at the wrong places. Or maybe, to use a metaphor that showed up in a chapter on supervision, the relationship between PhD candidate and supervisor resembles the parent-child relationship, and a certain degree of conflict, disagreement, or even trauma is unavoidable. After all, who would unanimously say that their parents have been 100% perfect? Maybe doing okay-ish is the best-case outcome as a supervisor or a mentor (and a parent).

But maybe we should also reflect on the way that supervision and mentoring is valued, and discussed, and taught in academia: in our opinion, much too little. After editing this book, we are more convinced than ever that as an academic community we need to change the way we approach these relationships. Instead of just treating it as a by-product of research, throwing both supervisors and PhD candidates in at the deep end and letting them learn (or not) the task while doing it, we should probably offer better training to all senior academics on how to supervise and to mentor. To establish clear guidelines on what is expected from both sides, and what is not. We've heard that some universities now do "supervision contracts" – probably that could be a good way to ensure accountability and protection for both candidates and supervisors. We feel that there is so much insecurity around this issue, with candidates unsure of what they can expect and supervisors unsure of how to handle this big responsibility. Making it a more central topic in academia, valuing the fact that it's hard work, and offering better training and a clear framework would certainly benefit everyone.

For the fourth and last observation, and going back to the bigger picture that we have tried to confront in this book project, an important lesson that I have learned while reading all the stories that were shared with us is how much community matters. Research, even on such a collective topic as democracy, is often a very lonely endeavor. This holds true for a first year PhD candidate as much as for an established professor. The best, and probably only way to not just survive but thrive during your PhD and beyond is to find and build communities. Communities of researchers that help you challenge and expand your notions of democracy, communities of peers that share your worries and struggles and victories, communities of friends and (chosen) family that support you in your private life. Without these, working in academia can be frustrating and alienating. So, if there is one

overarching advice to new PhD candidates that we can draw
from all the different experiences collected here, it is this one:
Find and build meaningful connections, do not try to do it all
alone. And, of course, talk about everything, don't be scared
to share your experiences. After all, that's what democracy
is about – creating a sum that is bigger than its parts.

We hope that this book project, in a very small way, can
contribute to making the PhD experience a little less lonely
and a little more democratic, for everyone involved. And,
as we already mentioned in the introduction, we want to
invite you, the reader, to share your experience as well. If
you want, share it with Chris and me, or with one of our
authors – our email inboxes are always open, and we would
love to hear back from you. Or share it directly with your
colleagues, friends, peers, mentors, supervisors, or students.
Tell your story, ask for other people's stories. Hopefully it
feels as empowering for you as it felt for the authors and us!

DemocracyNet

DemocracyNet is a non-partisan and non-profit association of and for researchers in democracy studies, who approach democracy from various disciplines and perspectives. It is located in Switzerland but has members around the globe.

https://democracynet.eu